The
GIFTS

The Revelation of the Spiritual Gifts in the Old Testament

ROYAL ROOTS PUBLISHING

California

Other Books by Huldah Dauid

Humbled by His Presence

Hidden in Plain Sight

Wisdom Builds

Little Judah in America

Her Peace of Mind

TO MY HUSBAND, TEACHER, & FRIEND:

לאדוני והבר׳ והמורה והאהבה שלי.
תודה על עמידתך לצדי ועזרת לי להביא את המתנה לישראל.
אני אוהבת אותך

CONTENTS

Foreword

The book you are holding in your hand is one of very few works ever written which has the true potential to elevate your spiritual consciousness and lift our Set-Apart Nation to a higher level of faithful functionality.

This manuscript, *The Gifts*, is currently one of the greatest works written on the subject of the "Gifts of the Spirit." This book does what no other book written on the subject of "spiritual gifts" can do because every other book concerning spiritual gifts is completely void of the original Hebraic perspective concerning the gifts given to us by our Elohim Yahuah. Huldah's naturally inquisitive mind led her on a compelling and insightful journey into the "Old Testament" origins of the spiritual gifts. Discovering that the spiritual gifts are Yah's Gifts to His children, the Nation of Israel, and their companions, is one of the most significant revelations of our time. In this book, you will see the missing foundational pieces of the spiritual gifts puzzle. *The Gifts* is written to truthfully connect the "who," "what," "where," "when," "how," and "why" of the spiritual gifts based in Torah. (*No other book that I know of, besides the Bible, does this*).

After over 35 years of studying, preaching, and teaching the Torah worldwide, I was becoming despondent over the so-called "Biblical literature" being produced today. Most of the writings are weak, anemic, worthless clichés being stewed and served to our people. The result of such feeble and frail efforts has resulted in a fainthearted and malnourished Nation. But this work is different. After reading *The Gifts* and working with Huldah in the final editing process, I realized that I was actually being enlightened and encouraged. For the first time in a long time, I received fresh insight and revelation concerning Yah's love (Ahava) which is His true gift to us. Working with Huldah on *The Gifts* also showed me how she is continuing to learn and grow as one of the most influential writers of our time. Huldah's writings always provide insight and clarity to important Biblical themes and doctrines. The clarity is accomplished by her constant drive to see the Bible as one complete revelation, revealed in one whole book.

If you desire to live transcendent and walk in the powerful paths of promise, then *The Gifts* is for you.

May Yah bless you on your spiritual journey to *be* a blessing to Our King Yahoshua and His Kingdom.

Shalom Aleichem,

Dr. Yoshiyahu Dauid Ben Israel
Moreh, The Awakening Remnant Koalition
March 8, 2021

Preface

It began, like all great journeys, with a question. It was December 2020 in Houston Texas at a retreat of pandemic proportions, and by that, I mean small and intimate. A perfect place for a seed to be planted. Out of what seemed like the blue H asked, "Huldah, what are your thoughts on the Gifts of the Ruach (Spirit)?"

Anxiety began to creep in, and my mind began racing, "she's going to ask me about speaking in tongues- Or maybe about prayer cloths- No, maybe it's about prophecy." As I tried to guess her angle I blurted out, "I have thoughts," and chuckled.

"No seriously Huldah," H persisted, "What do you think about the Gifts of the Ruach (Spirit) like tongues, intercession, etc.?"

I knew it was coming. If I had learned nothing else about this sister it is that she is serious about her answers, and because of the secluded retreat space, there was no avoiding the question. I took a deep breath and responded, "I believe in all the Gifts of the Ruach (Spirit), but I don't believe many have experienced or used them in their authentic function."

H had a perplexed but intrigued look on her face, "So you are saying that there is authentic gifting and inauthentic gifting?

"Yes," I replied. "Like real money and counterfeit money. They look the same but only one is approved and can be used as *legal* tender. In the same way giftings are counterfeited in religious circles because they are detached from the Instructions (Torah) of the Gift Giver. This "gifting" may look the same but can't yield true and sustainable results. True gifting doesn't manipulate the system and those who have it find their source in obedience to the Word of Elohim."

It was this initial exchange that led to an all-night conversation, a host of scriptures shared back and forth, and ultimately this work that you hold in your hand. In a bold question, at the right time, from a persistent individual I saw the Father's heart for unity and clarity as it concerns *His* gifts.

At the onset of the exploration of the Gifts of the Spirit, I was taken on a very extensive journey into my own unbelief. A personal decision 25+ years ago was limiting the Limitless and making finite the Infinite. I began to see my personal need for several of the Gifts of the Spirit and began seeking Yah concerning the activation of these gifts. This scared me. Had I been operating limited. Was I allowing the Spirit to lead me in some areas and not in others? Was my silent worship and holding back tears the residual effect of a hard heart and a closed mind to "more". I timidly began this journey like a child who had been caught red handed. Wide eyed and awaiting what I was sure to be a spiritual spanking. I began to confess my ignorance but seek the Father's face concerning his Ruach and the giftings.

You see, as a highly academic, fact-based believer, I operate in the seen, and while intrigued by the unseen, I either suppress or avoid what I don't understand. This allows for a safe approach to Scripture. My thought pattern is, "why do I need more than the expressed word?" The journey of studying the Ruach began as an academic search for information and quickly evolved into a spiritual journey. The responsibility to ascertain the Source of my existence, call, and service caused me to confront my "*doing*" versus my "*calling*". This also illuminated the severe limitations my unbelief and lack of faith were placing on Yah's ability to speak and use me to His glory. It also highlighted areas where I relinquished my call to those I felt were more "spiritually in tune" only to allow heresy and for lack of better words witches and warlock to use me and my platform to hurt the children of Yahuah. I found myself leaning on those who had the "gifts" that I felt like were important instead of asking Yah to equip me with the wisdom and gifting necessary to complete the task. I was like every person I read in the Bible who tried to pass on the torch of leadership because they perceived a personal deficiency instead of asking for what was needed to complete the task.

Now many will say I have seen the Spirit (Ruach) move in you. And while I cannot deny the reality that Yah has used me, I must admit that there were limits. These limits were due to my inability to commit to the rigorous mental and spiritual surrender necessary for a consistent outpouring or filling from His well of Living Water. I could only do so much before I felt depleted. Like a clumsy girl carrying water to her village, I was spilling what was poured in and left with just enough but never an overflow. I didn't how to contain or every properly use what I was being given from Yah. This left me keeping much of the light and insight I found hidden because I didn't trust the revelation or experiences that obedience in Torah was gifting me. I realize now that my issue was with counterfeit gifting found in the Christian church.

My first experience with the "Spirit of God" was terrifying! At 7 years old, with no prior explanation I visited a charismatic house of worship with a cousin who was baby-sitting me for the weekend. When we entered the building, it seemed to be like any other place of worship but once service started, I got the strange feeling "I wasn't in Kansas anymore". Whew chile was I right! I would learn that this place of worship was different than what I was accustomed to. The music began to play- The religious leader stood near the rows of seats and beckoned parishioners to come up for "prayer and healing." When the man would touch people, strange words came out of their mouths that I had never heard before. Individuals began running around the building and yelling loudly. In the front of the building there were people laying out for some sort of naptime. Others sat on a bench where they seemed to be waiting for something. I would later deduce through study and question that I was at a "healing and deliverance" service.

Many people fall all along the spectrum of religious experiences. This includes and is not limited to those where people have "experienced" God in a miraculous way. My experience is to in no way discredit the ability or the operation of the Spirit in individual lives; instead, it is to shed light on how circumstantial evidence is not the mode by which the Spirit operates. The Highest is not an Elohim of confusion and does not operate in only mysterious ways, nor is everything clear and cut. At the same time, His ways are not our ways. We have been given rules and guidelines to experiencing Him and the outpouring of His Spirit. Throughout this book, it is my goal to provide guidelines and perspective for those who wish to experience the fullness of the Spirit of Elohim and the activation of the giftings He has stored in your earthen vessel. This work is meant to reveal and realign the Gifts of the Spirit to the standard of Yahuah. I intend to show the heart and Spirit of Yah working in His elect and expose the counterfeit and inauthentic gifts to help Zion walk fully in their call to be lights of the world and salt of the earth.

> *As every man hath received the gift, even so minister the same one to another, as good stewards of the manifold grace of God. 11 If any man speak, let him speak as the oracles of God; if any man minister, let him do it as of the ability which God giveth: that God in all things may be glorified through Jesus Christ, to whom be praise and dominion for ever and ever. Amen.*
>
> **1 Peter 4:10-11**

1. Introduction

Everything in the universe is established by the *law*(word). of Yahuah

> *Through faith we understand that the worlds were framed by the word of Yah, so that things which are seen were not made of things which do appear.*
>
> **Hebrews 11:3**

Law is the replicable and fundamental truth of the universe that can be tried and repeated over an indefinite amount of time. The same is true of the fundamental elements which facilitate the activation of spiritual gifts. In this short discourse, I posit that the spiritual gifts among Israel are not operating in authenticity because of a lack of unity, misunderstanding of the gifts, and disobedience to the mandate to align with the *words of the Torah*. The spiritual gifts require the breath of Yahuah. His spirit (breath) exists in His Word. The activation doesn't work without an intimate relationship with the one from whom all blessings flow.

Stephen Hawkings, a well-known cosmologist, and atheist stated,

> *"Even if there is only one possible unified theory, it is just a set of rules and equations. What is it that breathes fire into the equations and makes a universe for them to describe? The usual approach of science of constructing a mathematical model cannot answer the questions of why there should be a universe for the model to describe. Why does the universe go to all the bother of existing?"*

What seems to be a profound question to Steven Hawkings is an easily answerable question to the believer. Rules found in complex equations are not just an attempt by science to address the "deeper" function of the universe. Rules to the student of Scripture are established to declare the Glory of Yahuah. When we obey the rules set in place by the Creator, we give meaning to why "the universe goes to all the bother of existing." It is in our existence that we show forth the Glory of Yahuah. The observable world is the tangible evidence of an Elohim who is working in and through His creation to bring about His expected end.

> *For the invisible things of him from the creation of the world are clearly seen, being understood by the things that are made, even His eternal power and Godhead; so that they are without excuse*
>
> **Romans 1:20**

While denying the existence of Elohim, even science understands that for something to exist and be conceivable, there must be a force or energy moving in a particular manner to produce something tangible. Ecclesiastes 3:11 states "eternity is bound up in the heart of man" and this is why such questions are asked.

There is an interesting contrast between King David and Stephen Hawkings. King David represents the mind of the children of Elohim, and Stephen Hawkings represents the knowledge-based approach to what is clearly above his pay grade. Both men are looking at their world through an observable lens. One marvels at the majesty of the Highest and the other is perturbed that rules seem to have personhood or necessity to express and exist. One man sees the expression as calculated and detached from a Creator, thus attributing the breath to a "*what*," while the other has found and located that "Who." Often in the quest for answers, humans tend to have an approach more likened to a Hawkings, filled with question and doubt, instead of reverent inquiry. It is the disposition of King David, that of awe for his Creator, which contains the keys to unlocking some of the most mind-boggling questions. The proper posture is that of a child asking a question to his Father. In this position, the complex becomes simple because the child is not trying to solve the problem but is awaiting an answer from his Father.

In Psalm 8, King David isn't questioning the existence of Yahuah as a non-believer; instead, his question is what does the Creator of the Universe have to do with lowly man and why has he been given a position of service

> *O Yah, our Master, how excellent is thy name in all the earth! who hast set thy glory above the heavens.*

> *Out of the mouth of babes and sucklings hast thou ordained strength because of thine enemies, that thou mightest still the enemy and the avenger.*

When I consider thy heavens, the work of thy fingers, the moon and the stars, which thou hast ordained; **What is man, that thou art mindful of him? and the son of man, that thou visitest him?**

For thou hast made him a little lower than the angels, and hast crowned him with glory and honour.

Thou madest him to have dominion over the works of thy hands; thou hast put all things under his feet:

All sheep and oxen, yea, and the beasts of the field;

The fowl of the air, and the fish of the sea, and whatsoever passeth through the paths of the seas.

O Yah, our Master, how excellent is thy name in all the earth!

With much humility and careful consideration, I submit that we are the vessels through which Elohim chose to breathe, and he has created this realm for us to express and live in a way that brings His name glory and honor. His breath has given us life, and in that life is the ability to live, move, and create with high potential, but that potential is only actualized if we are attached to our Creator and His Law. Through the Word[1] of His Law (Torah), we have wisdom, knowledge, faith, and healing. Through these six elements, we have the ability to operate as the Sons of Elohim.

---

[1] The Messiah is the 6th element. The Messiah is the word of Yah through which all the other elements exist. It was the authors choice to avoid redundancy and allow the Messiah to exist within the elements of the five listed fundamental elements.

This book's function is to address the "Gifts of the Spirit." In addressing the Gifts of the Spirit, we are going to explain their presence within the spiritual and physical seed of Israel. This book aims to shed light on the necessary elements required to activate the Gifts of the Spirit and unify Israel. Concisely, this work will cover what scripture teaches about the necessity of obedience, Messiah, and Torah-based function of all the spiritual gifts. It will cover the function of the Spirit of Elohim and the role of the Nation and their companions who have been called to operate in these gifts.

For the perfecting of the saints, for the work of the ministry, for the edifying of the body of Messiah: Till we all come in the unity of the faith, and of the knowledge of the Son of Yah, unto a perfect man, unto the measure of the stature of the fulness of Messiah: That we henceforth be no more children, tossed to and fro, and carried about with every wind of doctrine, by the sleight of men, and cunning craftiness, whereby they lie in wait to deceive; But speaking the truth in love, may grow up into him in all things, which is the head, even Messiah: From whom the whole body fitly joined together and compacted by that which every joint supplieth, according to the effectual working in the measure of every part, maketh increase of the body unto the edifying of itself in love.

Ephesians 4:12-16

14

2. The Sons of Elohim

In Hebrew, the term son is בן "ben" spelled "bet" "nun". Son in Hebrew is defined as, *"one who continues the house."* A son will show evidence of being attached to the house and lineage from which he comes. Every home has rules and customs that bind them to their family, and the same is true with the children of Yahuah. It is also important to note that those adopted into a family will also show forth the same evidence of being raised and dwelling in a particular home.

The children of Israel were admonished to have one Law, Torah (instructions for life) for the stranger and the home-born, making it easy to distinguish Israel from other nations.

> *One law shall be to him that is home-born and unto the stranger that sojourneth among you.*
> **Exodus 12:49**

> *One ordinance shall be both for you of the congregation and also for the stranger that sojourneth with you, an ordinance forever in your generations: as ye are, so shall*

*the stranger be before YAHUAH. <u>One law and one manner</u>
<u>shall be for you and for the stranger that sojourneth with</u>
<u>you.</u>*

Numbers 15:15-16

<u>*Ye shall have one manner of law, as well for the stranger,*</u>
<u>*as for one of your own country:*</u> *for I am   YAHUAH your
Elohim.*

Leviticus 24:22

*And if a stranger sojourn with thee in your land, ye shall
not vex him. <u>But the stranger that dwelleth with you shall</u>
<u>be unto you as one born among you, and thou shalt love</u>
<u>him as thyself;</u> for ye were strangers in the land of Egypt:
I am YAHUAH your Elohim.*

Leviticus 19:33-34

When a person sees the whole House of Israel, they should see
a direct reflection of the Master of the house. They should not
be looking at the Tribal factions or the race of the homeborn or
sojourner[2]. When Yah set the pattern for the identification of
His people it was not based in "race," rather it was centered in
attributes that pointed to His character. The Nation's division
and tracing lineage were to identify the family and tribe through
whom Yah's Salvation would come. What later becomes a
dispute is a direct reflection of the lack of love for Yah, and one
another, because of selfishness, sin, idolatry, and disobedience.
When we reconnect with Yah and align to Torah, we receive the
attributes of Yah's people. The attributes of his people are
rooted in their love one to another (John 13:35).

---

[2] Race is an issue because of intellectual and historical dishonesty. The present
issue of the race and identification of the Children of Israel is directly related to the
worlds inability to see the So-Called Negro as anything more than a slave. Racially
motivated conversations concerning Abraham's Seed does not exist because some
say they are Israelite rather it is due to the disregarding of the natural branches for
a white supremist narrative and replacement theology.

Love in Hebrew is אהבה which is formed from the root word אהב which means, "*to give a gift*." Israel's understanding of love is shaped by the *love* of Elohim. It is through Yah's expression of love that a precedent is set for an accurate expression of love.

> *For Yah so loved the world, that he gave his only begotten Son, that whosoever believeth in him should not perish, but have everlasting life.*
> **John 3:16**

> *If a man say, I love Yah, and hateth his brother, he is a liar: for he that loveth not his brother whom he hath seen, how can he love Yah whom he hath not seen? And this commandment have we from him, that he who loveth Yah love his brother also.*
> **1 John 4:19-20**

Since Yahuah's love sustains and endures so should ours. Having love one toward another is a testament of the One who is called Love (1 John 4:7-21). Love is not expressed only for a particular skin color and is not based in collective trauma. Love is a gift that has its roots in the love that Yahuah has first shown. The true evidence of Israel's love can be found in their ability to collectively assemble around the gift of love and unity which is a direct response to the accepting of Yah's gift (Deut. 6:4, John 17:21). This does not negate the natural seed but moves the qualification of nationhood to being one in Yahuah our Savior and away from personal boastings in the flesh (Romans 9:8).

Now that the foundation has been set for the proper understanding of the Sons of Elohim devoid of racial division, the current state of the House of Israel must be discussed. It is imperative that the issue of this present generation is not overlooked. Currently amongst the nations there is (and has been) the denial of the Natural Branches[3] of Israel. Similarly, there is much conjecture and unprofitable conversation regarding who is and who is not Israel. While the point of this book is not the historical migration of Israel and Judah, it is this authors opinion that the outpouring of the Gifts of the Spirit (or lack thereof) is due to disunity. And this disunity is found in the slanted narrative of nationhood, specifically the racial and migratory identity of the 12 Tribes of Israel. With that being said lets briefly look at the physical Nation of Israel and its function.

The Natural Branches & The Companion

The Children of Israel were originally set apart, as a physical People, to bring glory to Yahuah as an ensign to the nations. The Nation was originally comprised of the 12 Sons (tribes) of Israel (Jacob) who went down into Canaan during the great feminine in Genesis chapter 41. After 210 years in the land of Egypt Yahuah brought the SEED[4] out with a mighty hand and an outstretched arm as prophesied to the Patriarch Abraham[5] (Deuteronomy 26:8). The Israelites did not leave out alone but came out of Egypt a mixed multitude (Exodus 12:38-39). One Law was given to the home born and to the stranger that counted themselves amongst the Children of Israel. Due to the disobedience and the promise of chastisement for their rebellion the Nation of Israel has been scattered and the Kingdom of Judah dispersed. Israel was scattered into the nations surround the land of Israel (Assyria, Egypt, Pathros, Cush, Elam, Shinar, Hamath, and the islands of the sea (Isaiah 11:11)). The Children of Judah and some remnants of the

---

[3] Romans 11

[4] The SEED was promised to Abraham because of his obedience to Yahuah. It is also imperative to note that nations would be saved through Abraham's Seed. Although Abraham was responsible for the elected SEED and bloodline it was also promised by Yahuah that through him all the seed of the earth would be blessed.

[5] Genesis 15:13-14

Northern Kingdom of Israel were pushed down into the southern part of Mesopotamia and Africa after the sack of Jerusalem in 70AD. It was from Africa that a large group of Israelites experienced intracontinental slave trade by the African and Arab nations in the region which lasted for close to a thousand years (Ewald, p.465)6. Later the African Muslims were instrumental in the Transatlantic Slave7 Trade which gathered Hebrews and Israelites within the boundaries of West and East Africa and sold them to the European nations as cargo. It should also be noted that Israelites dispersed or were carried captive into the nations of the Gentiles including Rome and Greece during various occupational times in history including but not limited to the Maccabean period and the time period during the occupation of Rome in Jerusalem which began in 63 BCE and remains until this present dayi . These same Israelites also had children with foreign wives and husbands and those children being of mixed race have easily "integrated" or "passed" for those nations.8

The narrative is the Children of Israel, except for a European migratory remanent, are left from antiquity. The rest are "lost". The narrative of the "lost tribes" is LIE! The truth of the matter is that the nations have agreed to "lose" the Children of Israel. This conspiracy was prophesied in Psalm 83:5. Although Yah has chastised His children, He has not lost them. The book of the Prophet Isaiah states the Children are unlosable because

---

[6] Ewald, J. (1992). Slavery in Africa and the Slave Trades from Africa. *The American Historical Review, 97*(2), 465-485. doi:10.2307/2165729

[7] Those Jews who remained and escaped the trade can still be found as a remnant in this region today (Zephaniah 3:10). It is through the method of dispersion and scattering that we see Israel spread to the four corners of the earth (Isaiah 11:13) and they can be identified by their migration and the curses of Deuteronomy 28:45-46.

[8] i Wasserstein, B. , Prawer, . Joshua , Perowne, . Stewart Henry , Dumper, . Michael and Gordon, . Buzzy (2019, September 17). *Jerusalem. Encyclopedia Britannica.* https://Yahoshua.britannica.com/place/Jerusalem

they are inscribed on the palms of the hands of the Ancient One. Isaiah 49:14-22 states:

> *But Zion said, Yahuah hath forsaken me, and my Elohim hath forgotten me.*
>
> *Can a woman forget her sucking child, that she should not have compassion on the son of her womb? yea, they may forget, yet will I not forget thee.*
>
> *Behold, I have graven thee upon the palms of my hands; thy walls are continually before me.*
>
> *Thy children shall make haste; thy destroyers and they that made thee waste shall go forth of thee.*
>
> *Lift up thine eyes round about, and behold: all these gather themselves together, and come to thee. As I live, saith Yahuah, thou shalt surely clothe thee with them all, as with an ornament, and bind them on thee, as a bride doeth.*
>
> *For thy waste and thy desolate places, and the land of thy destruction, shall even now be too narrow by reason of the inhabitants, and they that swallowed thee up shall be far away.*
>
> *The children which thou shalt have, after thou hast lost the other, shall say again in thine ears, The place is too strait for me: give place to me that I may dwell.*
>
> *Then shalt thou say in thine heart, Who hath begotten me these, seeing I have lost my children, and am desolate, a captive, and removing to and fro? and who hath brought up these? Behold, I was left alone; these, where had they been?*

Thus saith Yahuah Elohim, Behold, I will lift up mine hand to the Gentiles, and set up my standard to the people: and they shall bring thy sons in their arms, and thy daughters shall be carried upon their shoulders.

This passage answers the question of Isaiah Chapter 1:

The vision of Isaiah the son of Amoz, which he saw concerning Judah and Jerusalem in the days of Uzziah, Jotham, Ahaz, and Hezekiah, kings of Judah. Hear, O heavens, and give ear, O earth: for Yahuah hath spoken, I have nourished and brought up children, and they have rebelled against me. The ox knoweth his owner, and the ass his master's crib: but Israel doth not know, my people doth not consider. Ah sinful nation, a people laden with iniquity, a seed of evildoers, children that are corrupters: they have forsaken Yahuah, they have provoked the Holy One of Israel unto anger, they are gone away backward. Why should ye be stricken any more? ye will revolt more and more: the whole head is sick, and the whole heart faint. From the sole of the foot even unto the head there is no soundness in it; but wounds, and bruises, and putrifying sores: they have not been closed, neither bound up, neither mollified with ointment. Your country is desolate, your cities are burned with fire: your land, strangers devour it in your presence, and it is desolate, as overthrown by strangers. And the daughter of Zion is left as a cottage in a vineyard, as a lodge in a garden of cucumbers, as a besieged city. Except Yahuah of hosts had left unto us a very small remnant, we should have been as Sodom, and we should have been like unto Gomorrah. [9]

---

[9] Isaiah 1:1-9

These Isaiah passages and others show that the love of Yahuah for the set-apart Nation has not waxed old. Rabbi Shaul (Paul) echoed these words to the Gentiles in the book of Romans when he states:

> *I say then, Hath Yah cast away his people? Yah forbid. For I also am an Israelite, of the seed of Abraham, of the tribe of Benjamin. Yah hath not cast away his people which he foreknew. Wot ye not what the scripture saith of Elias? how he maketh intercession to Yah against Israel saying, Yahuah, they have killed thy prophets, and digged down thine altars; and I am left alone, and they seek my life. But what saith the answer of Yah unto him? I have reserved to myself seven thousand men, who have not bowed the knee to the image of Baal. Even so then at this present time also there is a remnant according to the election of grace.[10]*

Scripture disproves a "lost tribe" narrative. The Word forces us to align with the heart of Yah for His people[11]. In like manner we will know those who are not the Sons of Elohim by their inability to love Yah's Natural SEED and those grafted in. If Gentiles don't have love for the Natural Branches, then they are not a part of Israel. Likewise, if the Natural Branches prohibit those seeking to be grafted in, they are counted with those who fail to align with the will of Yahuah and His Word. If the Gentiles don't have a heart for the blood-born Israel, they will be held accountable for the cursing of Yah's people, thus removing them from any chance at the blessing of Yahuah. This means that the perceived outpouring of any gifts into the Gentile nations are functioning counterfeit to the true gifting because true gifting is rooted in unification.

---

[10] Romans 11:1-5
[11] Romans 11:29

Today we have groups like Hebrew Roots and Messianic congregations who have the Torah and the Words of Truth yet operate with a White Supremist mindset concerning the scattered and dispersed of non-European descent. In like manner we have the blood born descendants of the diaspora who deny the grafting in of the wild branches (Romans 11:17). These individuals have taken up the personal responsibility of designating nationhood based upon the hew of Flesh. In all honesty both groups have missed the mark concerning Israel. The true called out assembly belongs to Yahuah and it is through His will and for His namesake (Psalm 106:8) that we are called and must not forget this as we seek to align and operate in the Gifts of the Spirit to the glory of Yahuah.

3. Authentic vs Counterfeit

Discord works against and ultimately delays the manifestation of spiritual gifts. The denominative mindset has the blind leading the blind. When people question spiritual gifting, it is not because they don't believe spiritual gifts exist, instead people are trying to connect their personal religious experiences with what they think the Bible teaches. They are looking for the gifts but are starting the quest from a defective foundation. The defective foundation is evident in the detachment from Torah.

People have a false idea of what spiritual gifts are because they don't know the Bible. Of those who claim to operate in the "spiritual gifts," are faking and lying-in regard to; healings, words of wisdom, discernment, and prophecy. This perversion of the gifts makes it hard to know who to trust. Everyone is quoting the Bible as their source, but the words are failing to bear fruit. All of this confusion is not from Yahuah.

Unfortunately, we see more unity as it pertains to wickedness in the world than we do unity amongst the righteous. It seems that we can find everything to divide over and very little that brings cohesion. We divide over dates, Feasts, and even the Set-Apart Language. These are the very essentials that should unify us and cause us to operate as one. This is why we will only see the true Gifts of the Spirit operating within the Remnant (those who walk with Yah and love one another).

Since very few people are operating in the authenticity of the gifts, we really don't know what true spiritual gifting looks like outside of the pages of the Scriptures. People have taken their ideas of the Gifts of the Spirit and have turned them into charismatic catch phrases and gimmicks in order to benefit themselves and amass financial "blessings". These individuals are outwardly inviting, but inwardly immoral and a part of the mass deception. 2 Timothy 3:5-7 states:

> *Having a form of godliness, but denying the power thereof: from such turn away. For of this sort are they which creep into houses, and lead captive silly women laden with sins, led away with divers lusts, Ever learning, and never able to come to the knowledge of the truth.*
> **2 Timothy 3:5-7**

Individuals with *evil spirits* (spirits of dysfunction) imitate the gifts and profess to do their works in the name of "*God*" but are truly led by an *evil spirit* which seeks to bring confusion.

> *These are wells without water, clouds that are carried with a tempest; to whom the mist of darkness is reserved for ever. For when they speak great swelling words of vanity, they allure through the lusts of the flesh, through much wantonness, those that were clean escaped from them who live in error. While they promise them liberty, they themselves are the servants of corruption: for of whom a man is overcome, of the same is he brought in bondage. For if after they have escaped the*

pollutions of the world through the knowledge of Yahuah and Saviour Yahoshua Messiah, they are again entangled therein, and overcome, the latter end is worse with them than the beginning. For it had been better for them not to have known the way of righteousness, than, after they have known it, to turn from the holy commandment delivered unto them. But it is happened unto them according to the true proverb, The dog is turned to his own vomit again; and the sow that was washed to her wallowing in the mire.

2 Peter 2:17-22

Signs, Wonders, and Oppression

In the book of Exodus, Moses was given the task to lead the children of Israel out of Egypt. As an accessory to Moses' call, he was also given the ability to perform signs and wonders. These signs and wonders were given to unify the Children of Israel and prove that Moses was speaking on the behalf of Yahuah (Exodus 4:1-9). When Yahuah began to execute judgment upon the Egyptians, He did so by the hand of Moses and through plagues. In the narrative it is highlighted that the Egyptian magicians were able to duplicate several of the plagues that Moses performed which aided in the hardness of Pharaoh's heart (Exodus 7:11-12). These Egyptian magicians were on the side of the slave master and the oppressor. This can be paralleled to the present, where institutions of religion teach its parishioners to disregard the Words of Yahuah in exchange for "blessings." These blessings are counterfeit mockery of what the righteous receive when they are obedient to the Word. The things people receive from joining with the oppressor serve as an aid to keep Yah's children in bondage. They do this because they know that freedom from oppression comes in authentic alignment.

Now going into dark magic and the power of Satan is not the purpose of this writing but it is a very true reality. There are ways through which individuals are able to circumvent the system of Torah, but it is not effectual long term. Eventually Jannes and Jamberes are no longer able to duplicate (Exodus 8:18-19) the signs of Moses and a huge distinction is made between the Hebrews and the Egyptians.

The ability to perform a "miracle" or to "speak a word" is not the same as having the Word of Yahuah inside and doing his will. It is hard for people to stomach the reality that preachers and religious leaders can be operating contrary to the Word of Yah. Experiencing "Anointing" on an individual or even the ecstatic worship of charismatic ministry is not evidence that Yah is behind it, it could be HaSatan and in most cases it is. In 1 Kings 18:20:40, the prophets of Baal came before Elijah and he made mockery of them and their gods. No matter how loud they yelled and cut themselves they were rendered powerless before the true Prophet. Most people today who are caught up in this religious entrapment don't realize the danger that comes in feeling based worship, because all the prophets of Baal were killed by Elijah. In like manner all false prophets and their followers will have their place in the lake of fire (Matthew 7:15, Revelation 20:10, Jeremiah 23:16). HaSatan presents as an angel of light, the wheat grows with the tares copying their form (Matthew 13:24-30), and many will say "Master, Master," I have done so and so in your name and he will say depart from me for I never knew you (Matthew 7:21-23).

> For such are false apostles, deceitful workers, transforming themselves into the apostles of Messiah. And no marvel; for Satan himself is transformed into an angel of light. Therefore it is no great thing if his ministers also be transformed as the ministers of righteousness; whose end shall be according to their works.

1 Corinthians 11:13-15

Proximity to truth does not make something true, just like knowledge does not become wisdom without application. That is why knowing the standard set in the word for gifting (and living) is so important. Many will find out what they *experienced* or *felt* as "Elohim" was the adversary at work. The Highest, blessed be he, is constantly creating a demarcation between Israel and other nations and it is imperative that His elect know what those boundaries are so that they are no longer deceived. In that same manner he has done so today by giving Israel rules to follow. His rules of engagement are clear distinctions which allow us to test the *spirit* of those who say they are His.

> *Little children, it is the last time: and as ye have heard that anti-Messiah shall come, even now are there many anti-Messiahs; whereby we know that it is the last time. They went out from us, but they were not of us; for if they had been of us, they would no doubt have continued with us: but they went out, that they might be made manifest that they were not all of us. But ye have an unction from the Holy One, and ye know all things.*
> **1 John 2:18-20**

Due to the curses that were placed upon the Children of Israel because of their disobedience. Many in the House of Israel and Judah have been led astray into non-Torah centered religions. In these places of worship, they have been exposed to what they believed was the *spirit* of "*Elohim*" or the "*Holy Spirit*".

Many would attest that they experienced the "Gifts of the Spirit" and have worshipped with individuals who were "truly anointed." In the "*Church*", irrespective of religious creed or denominational agencies, many were aware of *gifted* people without authenticity. For all intents and purposes of this study authenticity will be the word to describe those who are fully operating in the gifts of the spirit without circumventing the system set in place by Yahuah. Those with authentic gifting are those who operate both with the Law, Testimony, Messiah and understand that there is no separation of the Word. These authentic individuals are the ones who walk according to the same spirit as Joseph, Moses, Joshua, David, Daniel, and Messiah. These followers of the way have decided to hold fast to truth and refuse to deviate from the way of the righteousness.

Those who operate in inauthenticity are the individuals who will consult mediums, create religious ecstatic experiences, fashion new belief systems, and pervert Torah for a form of godliness but not according to wisdom and knowledge (2 Timothy 3:5). Many of these inauthentic individuals have carried their charismata into the house of Abba Yah and are passing off their religious foolery as authentic worship. All the while these characters are shaming the name of the Father and operating contrary to the prescribed path of Torah. This happens because the adversary has gone into the field and sown his own seed. Yes, Satan has seed. These tares have been encoded by their Father, Satan, and have "gifting" that is effectual in the disruption and confusion of elect. This may be hard to grasp because we don't fathom the world of unseen principalities.

> "For we wrestle not against flesh and blood, but against principalities, against powers, against the rulers of the darkness of this world, against spiritual wickedness in high places."
>
> **Ephesians 6:12**

If you deny the existence of principalities, then you will find it hard to understand how individuals who blaspheme and operate in *gifts* are able to do so. Every Eastern and Ancient Near East culture understands and believes in evil and good (opposing forces) which man can yield themselves vessel. Let this serve as a warning to all who maybe caught in the tangled web of the devil's deception.

The Manifestation

The word for manifest in Greek is "phaneros", which means "to bring to light." The equivalent Hebrew word is "galah" which means "to reveal and expose." The function of the gifts **reveals** who the true Sons of Elohim are and **expose** the counterfeit. Just the *ultraviolet light* is used for detection of counterfeit bills, Yahuah has given the *light of His Word* as a detector of all falsehood. The revelation of True Israel and his *Brilliance* is found in unity and the *manifestation* of the Gifts of the Spirit which works to make us one.

The first two gifts are Wisdom and Knowledge. They both deal with the mind and its condition. The mind is the main territory of spiritual battle. The mind is defined in the Hebrew as לב "leb," "*the authority within.*" The mind is controlled by words and actions. When the mind takes in words and actions of the adversary, which is his *seed*, then inevitably one will begin to behave in like manner. The adversary is fighting for the authority to command our lives and separate us from the Father. When we are separated from Yah, we are separated to the adversary (HaSatan). Once this happens a person is now Sons of Satan and will find themselves receiving his temporal rewards and everlasting punishment. (Scott, p. 89). The prince of this world has convoluted the gifting of Elohim and placed it into the hand of many counterfeit religions. The true Sons of Elohim are admonished in Scripture to be aware of those who profess to be led by the Spirt of Elohim but lack the evidence of the word in them.

There is a generation that are pure in their own eyes, and yet is not washed from their filthiness.

Proverbs 30:12

And though they say, Yahuah liveth; surely they swear falsely.

Jeremiah 5:2

For my people have committed two evils; they have forsaken me the fountain of living waters, and hewed them out cisterns, broken cisterns, that can hold no water.

Jeremiah 2:13

He that saith, I know him, and keepeth not his commandments, is a liar, and the truth is not in him.

1 John 2:4

For there are certain men crept in unawares, who were before of old ordained to this condemnation, ungodly men, turning the grace of our Elohim into lasciviousness, and denying the only Yahuah Elohim, and our Master Yahoshua Messiah.

Jude 1:4

Now as Jannes and Jambres withstood Moses, so do these also resist the truth: men of corrupt minds, reprobate concerning the faith.

2 Timothy 3:8

Now, Now, before we begin to point the finger of blame in one direction. The scripture also teaches:

For we ourselves also were sometimes foolish, disobedient, deceived, serving divers lusts and pleasures, living in malice and envy, hateful, and hating one another.

Titus 3:3

Even in the current disenfranchised state of the Natural Seed of Israel, Yahuah has promised that if they turn at His reproof that He will pour out His Spirit upon them and make his word known unto them (Proverbs 1:23). It is the knowing (intimate knowledge) of the word of Yahuah that is an important gift of the Ruach. In moving into our first gift, we must understand that Torah is not just obedience to laws but also a relationship with the one who gave the law. To take the gift and reject the relationship is dangerous. It is the relationship with the Gift Giver that causes us to understand the proper use, intent, and purpose of the gifts. The Gifts of the Spirit were first prophesied in the Old Testament as the attributes of Yahuah and the signs that would be on the Messiah and later handed to the nation of Israel as her dowry from the Bridegroom.

The Gifting in the Seed

When we look at the blessing attached to the man Abraham, we cannot deny the importance of a physical SEED (Galatians 3:16) One cannot expect to have the gifts of the family without joining the family to whom the gifts were given.

> *And I will bless them that bless thee and curse him that curseth thee: and in thee shall all families of the earth be blessed.*
> **Genesis 18:18**

> *And in thy seed shall all the nations of the earth be blessed; because thou hast obeyed my voice.*
> **Genesis 22:18**

All Israel seeking the blessings of Yahuah must unite under the same rules and laws that first caused the blessing to flow. The

Law teaches that seeds bear after their kind. To bear the fruit of obedience there has to be an attachment to the Source and obedience to His Law. Now, it may be asked what advantage it is to be attached to the family of the faithful if the blessing to Abraham would pour out to all nations. The issue is one of necessity and advantage. It's not either or its both. Without being attached to the Seed the gifts are not distributed. We see this example in Cornelius. Cornelius was a Centurion and a Roman who sought Yahuah. Yahuah did not adopt Cornelius and make a separate Roman family. Instead, Elohim worked on the heart of Cepha (Peter), a Hebrew Israelite, and used him to bring the Gentile Cornelius into the House of the Faithful. To be detached is a violation of the mandate for the stranger and the homeborn to operate as one.

Just as Abraham obeyed and was blessed, the proper functioning of the gift comes in obedience. Obedience is impossible without knowledge of the Standard (Torah) and the community (Israel). To deny the physical Seed is to deny a portion of the gift. The gift **is** the family because the family is where the gifts were designed to operate.

> *Ye stand this day all of you before Yahuah your Elohim; your captains of your tribes, your elders, and your officers, with all the men of Israel, [11] Your little ones, your wives, and thy stranger that is in thy camp, from the hewer of thy wood unto the drawer of thy water: That thou shouldest enter into covenant with Yahuah thy Elohim, and into his oath, which Yahuah thy Elohim maketh with thee this day: That he may establish thee to day for a people unto himself, and that he may be unto thee a Elohim, as he hath said unto thee, and as he hath sworn unto thy fathers, to Abraham, to Isaac, and to Jacob. Neither with you only do I make this covenant and this oath; But with him that standeth here with us this day before*

*Yahuah our Elohim, and also with him that is
not here with us this day*

Deuteronomy 29:10-15

*Men and brethren, what shall we do? Then Peter said unto
them, Repent, and be baptized every one of you in the
name of Yahoshua Messiah for the remission of sins, and
ye shall receive the gift of the Holy Ghost. For the promise
is unto you, and to your children, and to all that are afar
off, even as many as Yahuah our Elohim shall call. And
with many other words did he testify and exhort, saying,
Save yourselves from this untoward generation.*

Acts 2:37-40

*The promises were spoken to Abraham and to his seed.
The Scripture does not say, "and to seeds," meaning many,
but "and to your seed," meaning One, who is Messiah.*

Galatians 3:16

*For the gifts and calling of Elohim are without
repentance.*

Romans 11:29

36

4. The Gift

One of the main issues concerning the Gifts of the Spirit is translation. There is a remarkable amount of information lost in Biblical translation if not done accurately. When we see words in the Bible, they should be defined by the culture and the passage context. Unfortunately, there are many interjections of personal beliefs and modern culture into interpretations as one tries to unravel what it means to have the Gifts of the Spirit. Over the next two chapters, we will look at what a gift is and what it means to operate with the Spirit.

> Now about the gifts of the Spirit, brothers, and sisters, I do not want you to be uninformed.
>
> **1 Corinthians 12:1**

Most of the misconceptions about Gifts of the Spirit have been birthed out of 1 Corinthians 12. From this chapter, many have proceeded with their definitions12 concerning gifts and how

---

[12] [Gk *pneumatika* (πνευματικα), *charismata* (χαρισματα)]. Special gifts bestowed by God on individual members of the Christian community for the edification of the whole community.

the Spirit works in conjunction with these gifts. Spiritual gifts are thought to be a blessing, or something bestowed on a person to do as they wish, for their pleasure, but this is far from the truth. This is not merely a Greek error; it is an error of religious manipulation that seeks to use the gifts of Elohim for personal purposes. The Greek word for gift is more in line with the Hebrew definition than can be seen on the surface. To get this information, we have to know the Greek word and then take it back to its Hebrew root. The Greek word is charismata. Charismata is from the root word *charis*, which means favor and grace. The Greeks used a different word to mean gift (a present, something which doesn't require repayment), which is the Greek word δωρεὰ (*dorea*). The following verse uses both terms, and the English translator accurately translates the word for *charis* as grace while also translating the word for gift as gift.

Ἀλλ' οὐχ ὡς τὸ παράπτωμα, οὕτως καὶ τὸ χάρισμα· εἰ γὰρ τῷ τοῦ ἑνὸς παραπτώματι οἱ πολλοὶ ἀπέθανον, πολλῷ μᾶλλον ἡ **χάρις** (grace) τοῦ Θεοῦ καὶ ἡ **δωρεὰ** (gift) ἐν **χάριτι** (grace) τῇ τοῦ ἑνὸς ἀνθρώπου Ἰησοῦ Χριστοῦ εἰς τοὺς πολλοὺς ἐπερίσσευσεν.

But not as the offence, so also is the free gift. For if through the offence of one many be dead, much more the grace of Elohim, and the gift by grace, which is by one man, Yahoshua Messiah, hath abounded unto many
Romans 5:15

Yet when we arrive at the passage defining Gifts of the Spirit, the same Greek word is translated as gift.

Now there are diversities of gifts, but the same Spirit.

Διαιρέσεις δὲ χαρισμάτων εἰσίν, τὸ δὲ αὐτὸ
Πνεῦμα·

1 Corinthians 12:4

This translation conveys the idea that the gifts of the Spirit allow one to do as one wish. Because if something is a gift, it should be used as the receiver wishes. Interestingly the word gift is not a part of the Greek translation. This goes directly against the intended purpose of the gifts of the Spirit, which we to be used for the unity and establishment of the Assembly.

> *Praying us with much in treaty that we would receive the gift and take upon us the fellowship of the ministering to the saints.*
>
> **2 Corinthians 8:4**

> *For I long to see you, that I may impart unto you some spiritual gift, to the end, you may be established*
>
> **Romans 1:11**

> *Having then gifts differing according to the grace that is given to us, whether prophecy, let us prophesy according to the proportion of faith; Or ministry, let us wait on our ministering: or he that teacheth, on teaching; Or he that exhorteth, on exhortation: he that giveth, let him do it with simplicity; he that ruleth, with diligence; he that sheweth mercy, with cheerfulness. Let love be without dissimulation.*
>
> **Romans 12:6-9**

The word for gift used in each of these passages is the Greek word charismata χάρισμα (root word: charis) which translates as grace. The Hebrew equivalent for the Greek word is for grace is חן "hen." It comprises the two-letter root ח "het," נ "nun," which means to separate the seed. The het is the fence, wall, or separation between the seed and the outside of the house or protected place. The grace of Yahuah is not a gift of unmerited favor; instead, it is an invitation into a place of protection and separation from sin.

The Gift (Grace) is being welcomed into the house. The house is Yah's, and the rules are His. Unfortunately, sin has placed us outside of His house, but by grace, through faith, we are welcomed inside.

> *For by grace are ye saved through faith; and that not of yourselves: it is the gift of Elohim: Not of works, lest any man should boast. For we are his workmanship, created in Christ Jesus unto good works, which Elohim hath before ordained that we should walk in them.*
>
> **Ephesians 2:8**

By agreeing to enter the house, we agree to the rules of the house. There is no better example of grace than Noah for the intents and purposes of this chapter. The scripture tells us that Noah found grace in the eyes of Yahuah.

> *But Noah found grace in the eyes of Yahuah. These are the generations of Noah: Noah was a just man and perfect in his generations, and Noah walked with Elohim.*
>
> **Genesis 6:8**

This same grace moved Yahuah to give Noah the blueprint for the Ark through which the world could be saved. The Adherence to this blueprint was not optional. If Noah would have rejected the instructions of Yahuah concerning the building of the Ark he would have met the same demise as the rest of the world. Analogously, the gift of Yahuah to us is this same invitation (grace). Through the proper understanding of the gift, we see grace not as the ability to keep getting passes but as the prerequisite to joining those set aside for redemption. This gift, which is Yahuah's grace, allowed those who were willing to enter into his protection through the pattern found in his word. To create a new way or reject his method is to be left outside of the "house" when the day of calamity comes.

When Noah was instructed to build the Ark, he was told to do so publicly. Could it be that Noah's building of the Ark was a representation of Yahuah's grace and open arms to all who wanted to come in? It had to look strange to talk about a flood coming and building a boat that took 100 years with eight people. I believe Yah showed just how much space he had if only the people would agree to get in. The story of Noah has a tragic end for the unbelievers. The people mocked Noah, and by doing so, also rejects Yah and his plan of salvation. In my mind's eye, I can see them saying things like, you want us to get on there with you? Do you think Elohim is talking to you and no one else? Why should we join your family? If there is a flood coming, we can just build our own boat!

But then the rains came. What seemed like a crazy man preparing for a conspiracy theory of epic proportions was now a reality. As the first drops of rain fell from the sky for the first time, the faces of the dissenting crowd turned to panic. Noah was RIGHT! But it was too late. Scripture says that Yahuah closed the door because the judgment was coming.

The Hebrew word for the door is *dalet,* and the Hebrew word for opening or doorway is *patach.* The instructions given to Noah required him to smear and seal the Ark to make it waterproof. This also had to include the opening of the Ark that was three stories high. Let's look again at the English translation of the Hebrew text that mentions a "door" for the Ark based upon the instructions for building.

> A window shalt thou make to the Ark, and in a cubit shalt thou finish it above; and the **door** of the ark shalt thou set in the side thereof; *with* lower, second, and third *stories* shalt thou make it.

Genesis 6:16

The word for door here is the Hebrew word patch. Patach is an opening or a pathway. The pictograph of a pey is the picture of an open mouth or hole.

צֹהַר ׀ תַּעֲשֶׂה לַתֵּבָה וְאֶל־אַמָּה תְּכַלֶנָּה מִלְמַעְלָה **וּפֶתַח** הַתֵּבָה בְּצִדָּהּ תָּשִׂים תַּחְתִּיִּם שְׁנִיִּם וּשְׁלִשִׁים תַּעֲשֶׂהָ׃

The פתח (opening) was shut (*sagar*) by Yahuah, and it can be assumed without the implication that Yahuah kept the same pattern that he gave Noah to smear it within and without making it water (judgment proof). But before he could pitch (smear) the Ark, he had to shut (*sagar*) the people in. To make sure that we are not interjecting this idea of Yahuah sealing up the Ark or the portion that was still open. Let's look at the first mention of the word for shut-in scripture

> *And Yahuah Elohim caused a deep sleep to fall upon Adam, and he slept: and he took one of his ribs, and **closed up** the flesh instead thereof;*

וַיַּפֵּל יְהֹוָה אֱלֹהִים ׀ תַּרְדֵּמָה עַל־הָאָדָם וַיִּישָׁן וַיִּקַּח אַחַת מִצַּלְעֹתָיו וַיִּסְגֹּר בָּשָׂר תַּחְתֶּנָּה׃

Genesis 2:21

The word to shut in is shown as an action done by Yahuah. It shows that something, in this case, Adam's body, was sealed up as if it had never been opening. I posit that the same is true with the Ark. Yahuah sealed up the opening of the Ark and secured the contents seamlessly with kaphar. Kaphar is the same Hebrew word for atonement. The atoning (smearing) of the Ark was the final part of his redemptive work for the people who chose to obey him and enter into the vessel of salvation.

*And they that went in went in male and female of all flesh, as Elohim had commanded him: and Yahuah **shut him in**.*

וְהַבָּאִ֗ים זָכָ֨ר וּנְקֵבָ֤ה מִכָּל־בָּשָׂר֙ בָּ֔אוּ כַּאֲשֶׁ֛ר צִוָּ֥ה אֹת֖וֹ אֱלֹהִ֑ים וַיִּסְגֹּ֥ר יְהֹוָ֖ה בַּעֲדֽוֹ׃

Genesis 7:16

Yahuah, in the final moments before the judgment, applied the atonement to the Ark himself, as the door, and sealed up Noah and his family. This door closing was tragic for those shut out but a gift to those who accepted the invitation to reside inside the Ark of safety. Once the door was closed, those inside were safe, but those outside were set apart to destruction.

When most people think of a gift, they think of someone giving them what they want. When Yahuah provides us with a gift, he gives us what we NEED, the world needs to be saved, and only the one doing the saving knows what that should look like. Yahuah, in his infinite wisdom, put together the plan of salvation before the foundation of the world. There were no afterthoughts, and human error was already calculated. In His plan, he set aside righteous ones to replicate His character. He also set aside blood because to redeem; there had to be the currency for the transaction. After he provided the currency, He chose a family that he would covenant with.

In his plan, the family is the house, and the house's final detail is the door. In the same way that Yahuah was the door for Noah, Yahuah is the family's door.

> *Verily, verily, I say unto you, He that entereth not by the door into the sheepfold, but climbeth up some other way, the same is a thief and a robber. But he that entereth in by the door is the shepherd of the sheep.*
>
> **John 10:1-2**

> *I am the door. If anyone enters by Me, he will be saved and will go in and out and find pasture. The thief does not come except to steal, and to kill, and to destroy. I have come that they may have life, and that they may have it more abundantly.*
>
> **John 10:9-10**

Yahuah came in the flesh and became the door of redemption. He became the physical entryway through which all would have to enter if they wanted to be saved from the judgment that was sure to come. The gift is the door. The door is the sealer of fate. The door can only be entered through with the help and aid of the Spirit.

> *Now, this I say, brethren, that flesh and blood cannot inherit the kingdom of Elohim; neither doth corruption inherit incorruption.*
>
> **1 Corinthians 15:50**

It is through this gift(grace) that humanity has the ability to be adopted as sons. Any other way is not permitted. That is why those who seek after the father must do so in Spirit and TRUTH. If you reject the house and the door, you do not have the GIFT. The gift is the grace that brings you into the home and joins you to the family and its laws, the true treasure and blessing.

5. The Function of the Ruach

In the Hebrew language, the word for Spirit is רוה "ruach". "Ruach" comes from the 2-letter root רח "resh" "het," which means a *"prescribed path"* or *"to travel."* The origin of this word is nomadic; a shepherd would dwell outside the tent and tend to the flock creating a routine of care for the herd to ensure their health. The *good* shepherd knows that a flock thrives on routine. In the same way, the Spirit of Yahuah acts as the Shepherd leading Israel into Righteousness. The Ruach is the *BREATH* or, better yet, "the routine movement" of Yahuah working in his elect. The Ruach of Yahuah causes man to *move* on the prescribed path of Righteousness as laid out in Torah (Ezekiel 36:27). When the Saints in the Brit Chadesha asked if the people had received the Ruach (Acts 19:2), they were asking if the Ruach (Spirit) of Yahuah had taken up *residence* in their vessel and had enabled them to do the good deeds and follow the path of Torah (Number 14:24).

> *And the glory which thou gavest me I have given them;*
> *that they may be one, even as we are one: I in them, and*
> *thou in me, that they may be made perfect in one;*
>
> **John 17:22**

Now there are diversities of gifts, but the same Spirit. And there are differences of administrations, but the same Master. And there are diversities of operations, but it is the same Elohim which worketh all in all. But the manifestation of the Spirit is given to every man to profit withal.

1 Corinthians 12:4–7

There is one body, and one Spirit, even as ye are called in one hope of your calling; One Yahuah, one faith, one baptism, One Elohim and Father of all, who is above all, and through all, and in you all.

Ephesians 4:5-6

The very first thing that a person needs to activate the gifts is the indwelling of Yah's Ruach. The Ruach aides the individual in obedience with is the first step to activation of the Gifts of the Spirit. Obedience to the word of Yah is the first test of scriptural authentication. One should be looking to see if the individual professing to have the Gifts of the Spirit is functioning in agreement to the way (*or the path*) that Yahuah has plainly laid out.

True believers of the Bible understand that Scripture operates in a continuum. From Genesis to Revelation, there is an unbroken chain of information consistently reiterating the same thought in multifaceted ways to show the reader an overarching key point. These cyclical or repeating ideas are called motifs. We will use the motif of the Spirit and the gifts manifested throughout the Bible to present the reality that the gifts of the Spirit have an origin, and that origin is Yahuah, the Creator. Understanding the Spirit will provide the blueprint of Scripture which we will use as the core for alignment and activation of the Spiritual gifts. This alignment will serve as the foundation to admonish the Nation of Israel to strive toward oneness . This coalition will activate and authenticate the Seed and the elect of the Infinite One.

The 6 fundamental elements necessary to unlocking the spiritual gifts are *(this list is not in order of importance)*

Torah
Wisdom
Knowledge
Faith
Messiah
Healing (Rebirth, New life)

The Work of the Ruach

The Ruach is how we have been allowed to see the work of Yahuah in creation. The Ruach HaKodesh (set-apart Spirit) is Yahuah, expressed in action, or the energy of Yahuah. This same energy was the creating force in Genesis.

> *In the beginning Elohim created the heaven and the earth. And the earth was without form, and void; and darkness was upon the face of the deep. And the Spirit of Elohim moved upon the face of the waters.*
>
> **Genesis 1:2**

In the same way, the Ruach operating in the Called-out Assembly shows his work or movement to humanity.

> *For it is Elohim which worketh in you both to will and to do of his good pleasure.*
>
> **Philippians 2:13**

The Spirit does not operate independently. The Scriptures will always show unity between of Ruach, the Word (LAW), Yahuah, and His Salvation. The Ruach operating independently is unbiblical. The Scripture teaches that the same Spirit that was present at creation is Yahuah. This self-same Spirit is how all of the Old Testament *works* were made manifest, and it is the same Spirit that will show the elect the things to come.

> *Howbeit when He, the Spirit of truth, is come, He will guide you into all truth: for He shall not speak of Himself; but whatsoever He shall hear, that shall He speak: and He will shew you things to come.*
>
> **John 16:13**

Furthermore it is not, nor has it ever been, by the power of carnal man that we see the manifestation of Yahuah in His people.

> *Not by might, nor by power, but by My Spirit,*
> *Saith Yahuah of Hosts.*[13]
>
> **Zechariah 4:6**

Through the movement of the Ruach Yahuah has manifested himself in these last days and is once again activating the gifts of the Spirit through the quickening power embedded in the obedience to His word and the call on the Nation of Israel.

> *I will pour My Spirit upon thy seed,*
> *And my blessing upon thine offspring:*
> *And they shall spring up as among the grass*
>
> **Isaiah 44:3–4**

---

[13] Zec 4:6.

"And because ye are sons, Elohim has sent forth the Spirit of His Son into your hearts, crying, Abba, Father."

Galatians 4:6.

6. Torah

The gifts of Yah are poured out through His mercy and the first gift is Torah. Without Torah we would not understand the necessity, use, or function of the other Gifts of the Spirit. In the modern religious construct, we have experienced emulations of "spiritual gifts" without Torah and that has led to confusion, pride, and abuse of spiritual gifts.

> *"For Elohim is not the author of confusion, but of peace, as in all churches of the saints."*
> **1 Corinthians 14:33**

The gifts exist in Israel because the gifts are attached to the Torah, which is a forever. These are specifically for Israel (Spiritual and Physical). Through the covenant with Abraham Yahuah established His seed and promised to redeem them and make them a nation. It was in the process of becoming a nation that Israel was given her first outpouring of collective gifting from the Bridegroom. We see the pouring out of the Ruach (Spirit) on to Israel is in the Torah. When the Nation of Israel was brought out of Egypt, Yahuah began to pour out His Ruach to unify Israel and to establish His presence with His people.

This was done to help them do the work of the Law which he commanded.

> *And Joshua the son of Nun was full of the Spirit of Wisdom; for Moses had laid his hands upon him: and the children of Israel hearkened unto him and did as Yahuah commanded Moses.*
>
> **Deuteronomy 34:9**

> *See, I have called by name Bezaleel the son of Uri, the son of Hur, of the tribe of Judah: And I have filled him with the Spirit of Elohim, in wisdom, and in understanding, and in knowledge, and in all manner of workmanship*
>
> **Exodus 31:2-3**

It is also in Torah where we see the first outpouring of the Ruach. When Yah takes a portion of the Spirit upon Moses and gives it to the 70 elders. Here we see the *first* picture of what is known today as *"the day of Pentecost"* (Number 11:25). Through the motif of Yah's Spirit being poured out we find confirmation for the truths in the New Testament. This is not the first time that we are seeing these events, rather it is manifested in the New Testament as the fulfillment of the *divine* foreshadow.

> *And I will give them one heart, and I will put a new spirit within you; and I will take the stony heart out of their flesh, and will give them an heart of flesh:*
>
> **Ezekiel 11:19**

> *As for me, this is my covenant with them, saith Yahuah; My Spirit that is upon thee, and my words which I have put in thy mouth, shall not depart out of thy mouth, nor out of the mouth of thy seed, nor out of the mouth of thy seed's seed, saith Yahuah, from henceforth and for ever.*
>
> **Isaiah 59:21**

In Messiah we have a perfect example of the Word of Yahuah operating in the flesh fulfilling the prophecy concerning the covenant and function of the Nation of Israel. It is prophesied in the "Old" Testament that the Messiah will come in the fulness of the gifts and the Spirit of Yahuah. To avoid confusion, it is imperative to note that Messiah was not just a man who achieved enlightenment. Tout au contraire, Messiah is the Glory of Yahuah. He is the weighty visible portion of the invisible Yah, who is Spirit. Earlier it was stated that the Ruach is the movement of Yahuah and through that which is visible Yahuah does the work of showing His Glory. Messiah is the expressed Glory of Yahuah. He is the hand or the physical doing. He is how we see the doing of Yahuah's word and work. One might ask why we need a Messiah when we all have the ability to have the Ruach and operate in the gifts of the Spirit. My answer would be because you need Torah to activate the gift, but in our sin and trespass we have made Torah a curse rather than a gift. Due to the perfect nature of the Torah and our sinful nature Torah being just and perfect law necessitates the payment of blood for the remission of sin. In His (its) original state as written Law on tablets it killed us daily. So, Yah in His masterful plan put Torah into an Ark and then covered it with a tent of skin and caused it to dwell in the midst of his people. It was in that tent of meeting that Yahuah communed and reconciled the sin of His people (Exodus 25:16-22). You may be reading this thinking I am describing the tabernacle in the wilderness, but my intention was to show you just how parallel the dwelling of Yahuah in the midst of His people through the Messiah truly is. It was in the flesh that the law could die for mankind while also showing the perfection of Torah and be resurrected as the perfect example for Israel. It is the nailing of the Word to the tree that solidifies its power in us and fulfills the prophecy of the WORD being written in Israel's stony heart.

But this shall be the covenant that I will make with the house of Israel; After those days, saith Yahuah, I will put my law in their inward parts, and write it in their hearts; and will be their Elohim, and they shall be my people.
Jeremiah 31:33

For this is the covenant that I will make with the house of Israel after those days, saith Yahuah; I will put my laws into their mind, and write them in their hearts: and I will be to them an Elohim, and they shall be to me a people:
Hebrews 8:10

Torah without being *put* in the heart of man is spiritual, lofty, and unseen. It is when the Seed (Word) is planted into the soil of our prepared hearts that Torah becomes visible, seen, and physical. Until that point it is unattainable.

"But the word is very nigh unto thee, in thy mouth, and in thy heart, that thou mayest do it."
Deuteronomy 30:14

"But what saith it? The word is nigh thee, even in thy mouth, and in thy heart: that is, the word of faith, which we preach;"
Romans 10:8

What brings Torah to earth is the practice of keeping and obeying. Without Yahoshua, Elohim is high and lofty. The Spirit of Yah being put into Messiah brought the unseen into the seen and the intangible became tangible for the redemption of the bride and the fulfillment of the scripture which promised the Spirit of Yah would dwell with His people (Ex. 25:8, Ex. 29:45, Lev. 26:11, Ezekiel 37:27, John 1:4). Not just in us, but also with us as a representation and manifestation of His love FOREVER.

That which is unseen is now right before our eyes and undeniable.

The Torah was given to Israel as a spiritual gift but when they stopped keeping (doing) the works of Torah, the life that was in it was removed. This life was the Ruach, the spirit of Yah that aids man in the keeping the Law. Yah removed His spirit from man and they were left doing the works of the Law, without Him in mind, which is a curse.

> *And Yahuah said, My spirit shall not always strive with man, for that he also is flesh: yet his days shall be an hundred and twenty years.*
>
> **Genesis 6:3**

> *For it is impossible for those who were once enlightened, and have tasted of the heavenly gift, and were made partakers of the Holy Ghost, And have tasted the good word of Yah, and the powers of the world to come, If they shall fall away, to renew them again unto repentance; seeing they crucify to themselves the Son of Yah afresh, and put him to an open shame.*
>
> **Hebrews 6:4-6**

> *Cursed be he that confirmeth not all the words of this law to do them. And all the people shall say, Amen.*
>
> **Deuteronomy 27:26**

7. Wisdom

The Hebrew word for wisdom with begins with a two-letter root. This two-letter root חך comprises a "het" and a "kaf sofit" (final form). The "het" is a wall of a tent, fence, or separation and the "kaf" is the palm of the hand, to open. The combined meaning of these letters is "the roof of the mouth" or "the palate" (Benner, p.122). Over time the Hebrew word "חך" "place in the mouth" evolved into the, "place of discernment." When you add the third Hebrew letter (making the word a traditional 3 letter root) the definition changes to "desire", "wisdom", "and absorbing knowledge (learning)". This learning is not just the idea of picking up every book and eating healthy foods to make the brain function better, rather it is the training of the *authority within* to desire the word of Yah and His ways over everything.

The Scripture teaches us that wisdom is found in the word of Yahuah.

> *So He humbled you, allowed you to hunger, and fed you with manna which you did not know nor did your fathers know, that He might make you know that man shall not*

live by bread alone; but man lives by every word that proceeds from the mouth of Yahuah.

Deuteronomy 8:3

But he answered and said, It is written, Man shall not live by bread alone, but by every word that proceedeth out of the mouth of Elohim.

Matthew 4:4

Wisdom is the proper use of experiential knowledge. Wisdom can be likened to a place or pool that collects over time. Wisdom is the ability to judge and come to proper decisions concerning things you did not learn yourself. It is not just the accumulation of experiences, but it is experience by the will of Yah working in a yielded vessel to manifest truth and righteousness. In order to operate in this gift of the Ruach one must know where their focuses and desires could be leading them. Without wisdom people run the risk of being ignorant purpose and possibly in violation of the will of Yahuah. In modern society it is common to call individuals wise who have degrees and lettering but do not exemplify the wisdom seen by those who operated under the Spirit of Yahuah. Because wisdom was used to form everything and is the power of Elohim, those who are wise are attached to the Source of all wisdom. Now don't think that Scriptural Wisdom means a lack of intellect. It doesn't mean that a person does not have to study and work at wisdom. What it means is that the method (Torah) by which knowledge is obtained, and the teacher (Yahuah) are the sure path to advanced intellect in all fashions.

I have more understanding than all my teachers: for thy testimonies are my meditation.

*I understand more than the ancients, because
I keep thy precepts.*

*I have refrained my feet from every evil way,
that I might keep thy word.*

*I have not departed from thy judgments: for
thou hast taught me.*

*How sweet are thy words unto my taste! yea,
sweeter than honey to my mouth!*

Psalm 119:99-103

Wisdom Created the World

Wisdom was used to create the world. By speaking Yahuah
brought creation into existence (Proverbs 3:19, Isaiah 11:12).
Likewise, the Law of Yahuah was taught to Israel to be their
wisdom in the sight of the nations (Deuteronomy 4:5-6). In like
manner wisdom is not something that one can garner through
advanced age and knowledge, instead wisdom is something that
is gifted through the Ruach by the will of Yahuah. Solomon being
a young king prayed for wisdom instead of riches and is known
historically as the wisest man to ever live (besides Yahoshua of
course). Solomon's wisdom was limitless because he sought it
from on high, but when Solomon turned from the source of
wisdom, he experienced a decline. Solomon became as a fool in
his actions and goes down as a evil king in Israel (1 Kings 11:1).
Wisdom is not determined by one's prestige and when one
departs from the path of wisdom, as prescribed by Yahuah, then
wisdom does not remain with them. The wisdom of Torah
supersedes the wisdom of the world. It is from the Ancient One
thus it is timeless. By allowing the Living Word to dwell within
and making wisdom the primary focus of one's path, one can
begin to discern and be trained in all manner of gifting and
understanding.

Biblical wisdom is the cure for wickedness and folly. Biblical wisdom is joined with understanding (*banah*) and helps one to synthesize and conceptualize complex information and events. This process allows the induvial to make an informed and Torah based decision. This does not come from pure intellect but divine inspiration.

> *Say unto wisdom, Thou art my sister; and call understanding thy kinswoman*
>
> **Proverbs 7:4a**

The evidence of the spirit of wisdom is in the fear of Yahuah. Scripture teaches that before a person can be wise, they must fear their Creator and reverence Him as the One from whom all wisdom consists. There is a consistent nucleus in all the Gifts of the Spirit that is their ability and function to lead Israel in obedience. The fear of Yahuah is what helps Israel to live blameless, have wisdom, and judge righteously

> *The fear of Yahuah is the beginning of wisdom: and the knowledge of the holy is understanding.*
>
> **Proverbs 9:10**

> *Get wisdom, get understanding: forget it not; neither decline from the words of my mouth. Forsake her not, and she shall preserve thee: love her, and she shall keep thee. Wisdom is the principal thing; therefore get wisdom: and with all thy getting get understanding. Exalt her, and she shall promote thee: she shall bring thee to honour, when thou dost embrace her. She shall give to thine head an ornament of grace: a crown of glory shall she deliver to thee.*
>
> **Proverbs 4:5-9**

It is wisdom gathered through the fear of Yahuah that is our primary connection to the Creator. Once we have the fear of Yah and the proper palate or taste for His righteousness and he will begin to feed us with the goodness of this word increasing one's wisdom daily.

8. Knowledge

Knowledge in Hebrew is the word Yada (יִדע). To have knowledge of something means to be intimately acquainted through experience. Knowledge of Yahuah and one's calling is not achieved through worldly intellect, rather it is obtained through the "opening of a door" or "pathway by the hand of Yahuah," which allows us to see and experience Him and His will. Without the hand of Yahuah opening the door (portal) of our minds to know Him, we will never know ourselves. There is a popular esoteric statement that says, "if one knows themselves then they will be *free.*" Because man is created in the likeness and image of the Highest then his only opportunity at knowing himself and being free, is by reconnecting to Yah.

It is difficult to operate in knowledge void of relationship with the Knowledge Giver. Knowledge is necessary to exist and function in obedience to the will of Yahuah. Knowledge or knowing is the ability to understand and be intimate with your Creator and through that process we become intimate with everything around us. Hebrew knowledge is not something that exist in the mind, rather, knowledge exists in the *doing*. A Hebrew will never fully know what they will not practice.

Without knowing Yah and seeking our identity in his example we lack direction. Everything Yah Creates knows its purpose because its purpose is interwoven into its *being*. Science likes to call this *natural instinct*[14]. Natural instinct is defined as an animal's innate ability to operate in a particular fashion having never been formally instructed. This instinct is inscribed on to the genetic information of the created being and gives them the knowledge to operate as "designed." This same instinct is etched on the heart of mankind. The Scripture teaches that eternity is bound up in the heart of man[15]. Eternity is in man because he comes from that which is Eternal. Due to this higher connection, man by nature, is "hardwired" with the knowledge of his purpose. It requires a mustard seed amount of trust. This trust aids in the activation of the genetic information already inside. If we watch creation, we can see this trust at work. Spiders create webs in knowledge knowing how much web is applied to its geometric trap. The lion knows its territory and its responsibility to the pride. Atoms hold and bind together at the command of Yah to form molecules and cells. Everything under the command of Yah knows its function and purpose. Unlike nature who is willfully obedient, humanity fights against our Yah given function. No bird contemplates and fights its purpose of flight or migration. Likewise, we must be so sure, through a knowing of Yah's word and knowledge of His purpose in us, that we operate in obedience as if it is our *natural instinct*. Messiah, our example, was resolved in his life early because he knew and trusted Yah and he was not warring against the knowledge of his call or the Spirit within him.

---

[14] Merriam Webster defines *natural instinct* as a largely inheritable and unalterable tendency of an organism to make a complex and specific response to environmental stimuli without involving reason.
[15] Ecclesiastes 3:11

This wisdom and intimacy afforded Israel is called Zion's Treasure in Jeremiah 33:5-6. It is the combination of fear, wisdom and knowledge that allow us to rest assured in our salvation.

> *Thus saith Yahuah, Let not the wise man glory in his wisdom, neither let the mighty man glory in his might, let not the rich man glory in his riches: But let him that glorieth glory in this, that he understandeth and knoweth me, that I am Yahuah which exercise lovingkindness, judgment, and righteousness, in the earth: for in these things I delight, saith Yahuah.*
>
> **Jeremiah 9:23-24**

It has been prophesied that in the latter days we will not have to be told to know Yahuah (Jeremiah 31:34).

9. Faith

"Behold, his soul which is lifted up is not upright in him: but the righteous shall live by faith."
Habakkuk 2:4

The Hebrew word for faith is Emunah (אמונה). *Emunah* comes from the three-letter parent root, "Aleph" "mem" "nun" (אמן) pronounced *amen*. *Amen* is not a lip service but a practice and a way of living. *Amen* means something that can be depended or relied upon. The presence of the "vav" in the word אמונה, represents the "reliability" and "sureness" of one's faith. A faith so strong, that in the face of difficult situations or even death, the faith is unwavering.

Amen is also the confirmation of terms. It is knowing that a person is dependable and faithful in the fulfillment of their word. Yahuah is the perfect contract keeper. So much so that he goes into covenant with us, but the terms of the contract are upheld by his own veracity.

For when Elohim made promise to Abraham, because he could swear by no greater, he sware by himself
Hebrews 6:13

And said, By myself have I sworn, saith Yahuah, for because thou hast done this thing, and hast not withheld thy son, thine only son:

Genesis 22:16

When a contract or more accurately a covenant is set forth the surety of the terms are agreed upon in Western culture by a firm handshake. The handshake is intended to represent the firmness or dependability of one's word. For the Western minded individual a word is enough to establish a matter and unfortunately words can be used to break the contract as well. In the Eastern (Hebraic) mind, words are not merely words, they are life. When a person speaks words of agreement that begins the covenant, but the surety of the covenant is something that is tangible, which is why all covenants required the bringing forth of tangible elements. It was not enough for the Israelites to say:

And all the people answered together, and said, All that Yahuah hath spoken we will do. And Moses returned the words of the people unto Yahuah.

Exodus 19:8

They understood that "all that was said" and "all that they were agreeing to" had to be put into *action*. The action behind their affirmation was the evidence of their faith and the understanding of the contract through which they had bound themselves. Yahuah in His Infinite Wisdom requires faith or being attached to Him in order for us to operate in the spiritual gifts. He is the surety of the transaction. Yahuah is the one, in the case of Israel, who will fulfill the terms of the contract when we break it or fail to do so. When we attach ourselves to Yahuah we attach ourselves to bring **life,** but also our attachment and failure to abide has the ability to bring **death**. Not to us alone but also to the one who put Himself up as surety or (ransom) for our contract. When we survey the Scriptures with this lens, we have a much better understanding of what it means to take the name of Yahuah in vain. By saying we are attached to Yahuah we are using His name as "*surety*" and bring Him into covenant with our actions. It was the sin of the Nation of Israel (individual and collective) that lead to the trying and death of the WORD. Our disobedience placed a penalty (death) on us, and a payment was required a payment. It was the faith of our ancestors in the surety of Yah's ability to "pay our debts" that was the hope of the faithful. It was also the disobedience of us and our ancestors that led to the blood shed of the Word. Our faith has a dual effect, it can produce action that leads to salvation or it can produce death of the one who puts Himself up as surety when we fail to fulfill our side of the terms and agreement set forth in the Law. There is no such thing as a Biblical faith that is void of Torah.

To the Hebrew a man's (or woman's) word was made sure by the actions. These actions were backed by their lifestyle and their willingness to put their life on the line because of what they "believed." Seeing faith in the community has the ability to strengthen the community and to aid others in their establishment of their walk. This lifestyle of faith was represented in the cutting of a covenant, when two parties agree to certain terms there is a sacrifice of some manner which represents the binding of the parties through mutual agreement that only death can break. In the same manner when we are bound to Yahuah we cannot be bound by our lip service, but it is in the dying of self (flesh) that we are bound to Him in his eternal covenant. When we have faith, we are agreeing to be joined to Yahuah and leaving behind the former man. This means a death or burial in faith. And that same faith is what will resurrect us into the newness of life as Yah did with Yahoshua Messiah.

Faith is also understood and defined as truth. The shared two letter root word between truth and faith is "aleph, mem". The difference in the words is faith in its root form (אמן) ends in a "nun" and truth (אמת) ends in a "tav". Truth spelled "aleph" "mem" "tav" pronounced אמת "emet" is a declaration of that biblical truth is a whole account comprising the "beginning middle and end." The three letters in the root are the letters of the beginning middle and the end of the Hebrew alphabet which are the words by which creation was spoken into existence.

> *For by him were all things created, that are in heaven, and that are in earth, visible and invisible, whether they be thrones, or dominions, or principalities, or powers: all things were created by him, and for him: And he is before all things, and by him all things consist.*
>
> **Col 1:16–17**

One cannot believe that the Word of Yahuah is true and deny the validity or power of the Law of Elohim. One of the attributes of Yahuah is *Truth*. He is Truth, so to deny the Creator is to deny *truth*.

> *And Yahuah passed by before him, and proclaimed, Yahuah, Yahuah Elohim, merciful and gracious, longsuffering, and abundant in goodness and truth, keeping mercy for thousands, forgiving iniquity and transgression and sin, and that will by no means clear the guilty, visiting the iniquity of the fathers upon the children, and upon the children's children, unto the third and to the fourth generation. And Moses made haste, and bowed his head toward the earth, and worshipped.*
>
> **Exodus 34:6-8**

The declaration of the Truth of Yahuah has a powerful effect on those who have attached themselves to Yahuah. Truth leads to *worship*. When Yahuah declared His nature to Moses he made haste and bowed his head and worshipped. There is a strong correlation between faith, truth, and worship.

When a person desires to operate in the Gifts of the Spirit, especially the gift of *faith*, that individual is attaching themselves to *truth*. When one deviates from the path of truth there will always be evidence of it in their inability to authentically operate in their gifts. To see a functional example of this one does not have to look far. In the house of Judah and Israel you see an abundance of gifting and talent, but those gifts are constantly used for the glorification of self and systems that replicate oppression within the Nation of Israel. If Yahuah is not at the center than the gift will be exchanged for bondage and the truth will be turned into a lie (Romans 1:25, Isaiah 5:20). Those who desire the gifts have to be extremely careful that the *truth of the word* and the expectation of Yahuah are the guiding factors in the operation and function of the gift.

Faith is a very unique spiritual gift that many seem to profess. But when you bring in the Hebraic definition of faith, we find that there is a lack of faith in the "faith" community. When Messiah asked will he find faith when the son of man returns (Luke 18:8), he was asking if he is going to find anyone connected to the truth of faith in Torah. This is because everyone was going toward the tradition of man and away from the Word of Yahuah.

Faith and Worship

It seems like everyone is ready to place themselves as surety for their profession not knowing that surety requires a payment. What is the payment or the end result of faith? Well for many this won't be good news (pun intended) but the payment for faith is worship and worship is synonymous with death. Let's take a closer look at the correlation between faith and death.

The Hebrew word for worship is *shachah*. It comes from the two-letter root word שח "shin" "het" which means, "to sink deep as going into a pit." The 3-letter root שחה "shin" "het" "hey" ends in a "hey" which is also representative of breath, specifically the Breath of Yahuah. This gives the idea that worship is not just "to sink down into a pit" or "to bow," but to have the Breath (Ruach) of Yahuah *breathed* into you and resurrect you to new life. This also can be understood as a new life which reveals who you are attached to.

Abraham and Sarah were perfect examples of individuals with gift faith who sought out and walked before Yahuah. He breathed His breath into them and revealed Himself to them. Both Abram(ham) and Sara(h) had the letter "hey" added to their names after they were identified as the vessels through whom Yahuah would perform His great work of nation building and blessing. Abraham believed in what Yahuah said. He lived out what was told to him and was *sure* in it. (Emunah) Faith breeds action when belief and worshipped are joined together. One of the most easily identifiable examples of faith and worship is when Abraham takes the son of the promise, Isaac, up on Mount Moriah to *worship* Yahuah. In the historical account Abraham takes Isaac up to sacrifice with the thought that he is supposed to sacrifice Isaac to Yahuah. Now this was not just a situation of death, but it was fully believed in the mind of Abraham that his *worship* and obedience would cause Isaac to be resurrected (Hebrews 11:19). Our call is to be like Abraham who believed Yahuah has the power to perform His will. It is through *faith* that the believer is established in their relationship with their Creator. Abraham understood that his faith was imperative to the expected outcome. Likewise, to desire the gifts of the spirit means both action and understanding that the things which have not been made manifest could be due to our lack of secure attachment to the Gift Giver. We could be missing the mark of sinking down into the pit and dying to self. Our task is not just one of intellectually accepting the ways of Yahuah, instead we are called to a lifestyle of *worship* and *faith*. The two together show the establishment of the gift of the Ruach because without the Ruach it is impossible to walk upright before Yah and to endure to the end (Romans 8:8). All of those counted as faithful (the patriarchs and matriarchs) listed in the "Hall of Faith" (Hebrews 11), show us faith as a lifestyle. I think it is important to note during the reading of Hebrews chapter 11 that we see the death in conjunction with faith. This was not a death to be feared, but a death of one who is awaiting the promise (Revelation 2:10). These individuals believed in a day to come and *One* to come who would establish their faith, be surety for their souls, and testify of the truth that they believed in. Each person in the "Hall of Faith" is an example of how Israel *is* to walk in the gifting of faith.

We see the culmination and the expectation of faith in Yahoshua. He was so sure that he was willing to go down to the pit (grave) through death on a tree with the unwavering "belief" that he would be resurrected

> *For as Jonas was three days and three nights in the whale's belly; so shall the Son of man be three days and three nights in the heart of the earth.*
> **Matthew 12:40**

> *From that time forth began Yahoshua to shew unto his disciples, how that he must go unto Jerusalem, and suffer many things of the elders and chief priests and scribes, and be killed, and be raised again the third day.*

Matthew 16:21

The Son of Man must be delivered into the hands of sinful men, and be crucified, and on the third day rise again.

Luke 24:7

Yahoshua answered, "Destroy this temple, and in three days I will raise it up again."

John 2:19

that He was buried, that He was raised on the third day according to the Scriptures

1 Corinthians 15:4

The same faith that Messiah had through the Ruach is available to each of those who agree to walk according to his way. Scripture tells us that if we walk as Messiah walked and be buried with him then we have the same ability to becalled sons of Yah and the full blessing of faith, endurance, and most importantly resurrection.

In whom also ye are circumcised with the circumcision made without hands, in putting off the body of the sins of the flesh by the circumcision of Messiah: Buried with him in baptism, wherein also ye are risen with him through the faith of the operation of Elohim, who hath raised him from the dead. And you, being dead in your sins and the uncircumcision of your flesh, hath he quickened together with him, having forgiven you all trespasses; Blotting out the handwriting of ordinances that was against us, which was contrary to us, and took it out of the way, nailing it to his cross; And having spoiled principalities and powers, he made a shew of them openly, triumphing over them in it.

Colossians 2:11-15

Therefore, we are buried with him by baptism into death: that like as Messiah was raised up from the dead by the glory of the Father, even so we also should walk in newness of life. For if we have been planted together in the likeness of his death, we shall be also in the likeness of his resurrection: Knowing this, that our old man is crucified with him, that the body of sin might be destroyed, that henceforth we should not serve sin.

Romans 6:4

SIMON Peter, a servant and an apostle of Yahoshua Messiah, to them that have obtained like precious faith with us through the righteousness of Elohim and our Saviour Yahoshua Messiah

2 Peter 1:1

For ye are dead, and your life is hid with Messiah in Elohim.

Colossians 3:3

When we are securely fastened to the Source, we will be resurrected as new creatures in both this world and the world to come. Our faith that causes us to walk before Yahuah and to be securely attached is the greatest gift to our brothers and sisters in the faith. Faith is not for our own personal boasting. Faith is a gift and a sign of the gathering of Yahuah. Those who are gathered to Yahuah are brought in through the faith and surety of Yahuah.

10. The Messiah

The first question that must be answered is where does one find the Messiah in the Old Testament? Many people think that the Messiah is a new testament concept created by the catholic church to aid in the decimation of the Israelite people. Even amongst those who believe in a Messiah there is contention over who the Messiah is. And of the group as a whole there are those who believe the words of Scripture but still struggle with the articulation of who Messiah is because "they" cannot see the Messiah in the "Old Testament". I submit that people struggle with seeing the Messiah in the Old Testament because they don't read *His* book or because they don't know what to look for when they are reading from "the volume of the book that speaks of Him".

> Then I said, "Here I come in the scroll of the book of the writings of me".
>
> **Psalm 40:7**

The verse that proceeds this declaration talks about the opening of the ear of the One who is coming (Psalm 40:6). In Hebrew "the opening of the ear" is the cultural practice related to designating or binding a servant to a house. When a servant wished to stay and continue to dwell with his master, he or she essentially offered their body (person/self) as a vessel for that home forever (Exodus 21:6). Likewise, the Messiah was a chosen vessel before the foundation of the earth that was willing to serve the Nation. (1 Peter 1:20) The body of Messiah was not first seen in the new testament, but a shadow (a copy of what was already in Shamayim (Hebrews 8:5)) was seen all throughout the scripture in the expression of Yahuah's Glory (Isaiah 40:5). The body was made manifest and revealed in the Brit Chadesha on the mount of transfiguration where the connection to Yahuah's Glory in the Old Testament and the manifestation of His Glory in the physical body of Yahoshua were brought seamlessly.

Will Yah be Physically Amongst Israel?

But will Elohim indeed dwell with man upon the earth? Even heaven, the highest heaven, cannot contain You, much less this temple I have built.

1 Chronicles 6:18

For thus says the One who is high and lifted up, who inhabits eternity, whose name is Holy: "I dwell in a high and holy place, and with the oppressed and humble in spirit, to restore the spirit of the lowly and revive the heart of the contrite.

Isaiah 57:15

And they are to make a sanctuary for Me, so that I may dwell among them.

Exodus 25:8

And I will dwell among the children of Israel, and will be their Elohim.

Exodus 29:45

I will walk among you and be your Elohim, and you will be My people.

Leviticus 26:12

Therefore Yahuah himself shall give you a sign; Behold, a virgin shall conceive, and bear a son, and shall call his name Immanuel.

Isaiah 7:14

For unto us a child is born, unto us a son is given, and the government will be upon His shoulders. And He will be called Wonderful Counselor, Mighty Elohim, Everlasting Father, Prince of Peace.

Isaiah 9:6

In the beginning was the Word, and the Word was with Elohim, and the Word was Elohim. The same was in the beginning with Elohim. And the Word was made flesh, and dwelt among us, (and we beheld his glory, the glory as of the only begotten of the Father,) full of grace and truth.

John 1:1-2,14

But I tell you that something greater than the temple is here.

Matthew 12:6

For there to be a Messiah to the nation this Messiah has to be Yahuah. We know from the above verses that Yahuah is the One who is going to dwell amongst the people. We also know that Yahuah does not give His Glory to another. In the Hebrew language the function of a king is one who walks amongst the people and the function of a savior is one who saves or rescues.

Both refer to physical action which we have seen Yah perform at the hand of His Messenger (Himself). We see how Yah has appeared to the people standing (yes with feet) in the door of the tabernacle and on the ground like sapphire before the 70 elders (Exodus 24:9. The testimony of the "Old Testament" is that Elohim is Spirit, but He has also revealed Himself in *person* to His people.

Yahuah designated a specific body for the expression of His person and this *person* can be seen from the Garden of Eden until the End of the Book of Revelation. If we take the words of Scripture literally (at their peshat (literal) level) we cannot deny that there is a physical expression of Yahuah in the words of Tanakh. Every time someone physically sees Yahuah in the Scriptures we are seeing Yahoshua. Many theological circles try and explain the physical presence of Yah away as *anthropomorphic* to propagate the thought that Jesus (Yahoshua) in the New Testament is a new manifestation, with new rules, and a new way. But any Bible student worth their salt knows that Yahoshua was prophesied and appeared to several of the biblical patriarchs by his own profession.

The Man walking in the garden (He also prepared the first sacrifice and gave skins to Adam and Chawah (Eve)) (Genesis 3:21).
The Man who appeared16 to Abraham (Genesis 18, John 8:55-57).
Jacob wrestled with a Man at Penuel (Genesis 32:30)
The Man in the midst of the burning bush (Exodus 3:2)
Moses speaks face to face with Yahuah and sees *His* form (Numbers 12:8)
The Man who descends in the cloud and stands in the tabernacle door (exodus 34:5)

---

16 Earlier in Genesis 17 Yahuah appeared to Abraham declaring who he is. This is why there should be no confusion as to who is before him.

The man who stood before the 70 elders (Exodus 24:10-11)
The man in the fiery furnace with Mishael, Hananiah, Azariah
(Daniel 3:25)

As the savior of Israel, Yahuah brought His salvation in His own
name, Yahoshua ("Yah" is "Shua") fulfilling His words that He is
Savior and there is none beside Him.

> *I am Yahuah; that is My name! I will not yield My glory to
> another or My praise to idols.*
>
> **Isaiah 42:8**

> *For I am Yahuah your Elohim, the Holy One of Israel, your
> Savior; I give Egypt for your ransom, Cush and Seba in
> your place.*
>
> **Isaiah 43:3**

> *Speak up and present your case--yes, let them take
> counsel together. Who foretold this long ago? Who
> announced it from ancient times? Was it not I, Yahuah?
> There is no other Elohim but Me, a righteous Elohim and
> Savior; there is none but Me.*
>
> **Isaiah 45:21**

> *You will drink the milk of nations and nurse at the breasts
> of royalty; you will know that I, Yahuah, am your Savior
> and your Redeemer, the Mighty One of Jacob.*
>
> **Isaiah 60:16**

Yahuah as Savior is not a "New Testament" concept but as Brad
Scott once said it is just TRUE. Not only has Yah been the savior
of Israel but the concept of paying the price with His Passover
sacrifice (Exodus 12:11) (A blood sacrifice (Leviticus 17:11)) is
not new either. I will conclude the testifying of messiah with
these last two verses which I hope will help the nation of Israel

begin to see the seamless salvation and the fulfillment of scripture in their Messiah.

> *Fear and dread shall fall upon them; by the greatness of thine arm they shall be as still as a stone; till thy people pass over, O YahUAH, till the people pass over, which thou hast purchased.*
>
> **Exodus 15:6**

> *Take heed therefore unto yourselves, and to all the flock, over the which the Holy Ghost hath made you overseers, to feed the church of Elohim, which He hath purchased with **His own blood**.*
>
> **Acts 20:28**

The blood of the lamb allowed Yahuah to pause his judgment so that the people of Israel could Passover into the promise safely. This same method of redemption is also found in his purchase of His Bride in full. When the Word was nailed to the tree once and for all the fulfillment of the prepared vessel, salvation, and the bride dowry were secured. It was in the resurrection and the gifting of the Ruach that Israel once again was restored. It is in this restoration that the dowry of the spiritual gifts was poured out to make us a nation of *Light Bearers* and allows us to walk in obedience to His Laws, Statutes, and Commandments. This is the true evidence of our salvation.

11. Healing

The healing of the Nation of Israel is a miracle of most endearing proportions. For the Creator of Heaven and Earth to see and meet the needs of His people shows how imperative it is that the gifts of the spirit reside in whole vessels. One of the most neglected practices and perquisites to service and worship is healing. Many people have been hurt more than they have been healed in community which is contrary to the function of a unified Nation. It is unfortunate that healing before ministering is overlooked or practiced in superficial ways. Many talented and gifted individuals wishing to serve Yahuah are used for their gifting but are serving marred, traumatized, and empty. People are quick to use the gifting but are slow to participate in the healing processed. Being called is the beginning of the healing process, but the actual healing is directly attached to the words of Elohim. In the Hebraic lifestyle there was a mandate of the reading of the words of the Law to the people as well as the copying of the words of the Law by the kings. Through this mandate of continually washing in the word, both the king and the people were a part of a communal process that promoted a holistic life. The body (a community) cannot operate in the capacity of its gifting without the Law and the healing. In this section we will look at: healing by light, healing by loosening, healing by words, and healing by the Messiah.

> *Yahoshua answered, "It is not the healthy who need a doctor, but the sick.*
>
> **Luke 5:31**

Healing by Light

Light in Hebrew is אור "Or". "Or" is defined as "light" or Brightness". When Yahuah spoke in Genesis 1:3 bringing "or"der to chaos he said " let there be light (אור). Light was and still is the antidote for disorder. **The Word of Yah is Light**. Light was used to bring forth fruit bearing seed and herbs. These fruit and herbs were the evidence of the healing of the land and likewise they can be used to heal the body of humanity that was formed from the ground. However, before the fall there was no sickness and disease. Sickness is a natural consequence of disobedience. When man ate of the fruit of the Tree of Knowledge of Good and Evil a different type of chaos came forth which put the body into a state of decay. "Dis"ease is a result of dis"or"der. The *order* that Yahuah brought to the former chaos with the Light of His Word was once again set in disarray. Darkness/Disorder causes death and the word of Yahuah brings Light/Order.

> For the commandment is a lamp; and the law is *light*; and reproofs of instruction are the way of life:
>
> **Proverbs 6:23**

*But unto you that fear my name shall the **Sun** of*
*righteousness arise with **healing** in his wings; and ye*
shall go forth and grow up as calves of the stall.

Malachi 4:2

Thy dead men shall live,
Together with my dead body shall they arise.
Awake and sing, ye that dwell in dust:
For thy dew is as the dew of herbs (אורה),
And the earth shall cast out the dead.

Isaiah 26:19

Herbs in the verse above is translated from the Hebrew word
אורה "Orah". "Orah" shares the same root as "Light" (אור). Herbs
are grown from seed, burial (in fertile soil), light, and breath
(Ruach). The same is true for the process of healing the physical
and spiritual body of man.

Give ear, O ye heavens, and I will speak;
And hear, O earth, the words of my mouth.
My doctrine shall drop as the rain,
My speech shall distil as the dew,
*As the small rain upon the tender **herb**,*
And as the showers upon the grass:
Because I will publish the name of the Lord:
Ascribe ye greatness unto our God.
He is the Rock, his work is perfect:
For all his ways are judgment:
A God of truth and without iniquity,
Just and right is he.

Deuteronomy 32:2, directly connects the teaching and speech
of Yahuah to the dropping of dew and rain upon the herb (which
heals). Yahuah gives the water and light that produces the herb
which heals the body. Yahuah spoke His Word that became flesh
and bore the fruit that heals and resurrects the soul. Likewise,

light quickens, brings life (היה), to dead bodies as dew does plants. The Light of Yahuah is the healing that quickens the *Seed* within us. Quickening means to make alive (revive). The Light of Yah is what heals and brings us up from the depths of the earth, once we submit to His order.

> *Thou, which hast shewed me great and sore troubles,*
> *Shalt quicken me again,*
> *And shalt bring me up again from the depths of the earth.*
> **Psalm 71:20**

Just as chaos turned to order by the illuminating Light in Genesis 1:3, correspondingly, the Light of Elohim quickens to bring His Light to the nations through obedience and fruit-bearing.

> *My soul cleaveth unto the dust: quicken thou me according to thy word.*
> **Psalm 119:25**

> *Behold, I have longed after thy precepts: quicken me in thy righteousness.*
> **Psalm 119: 40**

> *This is my comfort in my affliction: for thy word hath quickened me.*
> **Psalm 119: 50**

> *I am afflicted very much: quicken me, O Yahuah, according unto thy word.*
> **Psalm 119:107**

> *For as the Father raiseth up the dead, and quickeneth them; even so the Son quickeneth whom he will.*

John 5:21

(As it is written, I have made thee a father of many nations,) before him whom he believed, even Elohim, who quickeneth the dead, and calleth those things which be not as though they were.

Romans 4:17

For the bread of Elohim is he which cometh down from heaven, and giveth life unto the world.

John 6:63

Healing is a form of resurrection when a person is sick unto death. When the healer revives them, they have new life. The same is true when one is sick unto death because of sin. It is the word of Yah that quickens the body.

And you hath he quickened, who were dead in trespasses and sins;

Wherein in time past ye walked according to the course of this world, according to the prince of the power of the air, the spirit that now worketh in the children of disobedience: Among whom also we all had our conversation in times past in the lusts of our flesh, fulfilling the desires of the flesh and of the mind; and were by nature the children of wrath, even as others. But God, who is rich in mercy, for his great love wherewith he loved us, even when we were dead in sins, hath quickened us together with Christ, (by grace ye are saved;)

Ephesians 2:1-5

Healing by Loosening

Another word for healing is the Hebrew word רפא "rapha." "Rapha" means to "heal" and "loosen from pain." Rapha is the movement or the act of curing through stitching or repairing a breech. In the Near East rugs and fabric was repaired by loosening the frayed or torn fabric and restoring it to its former wholeness. In the same way Yahuah uses the healing and the reset in his word, feast, and in fasting to loosen the bonds of demon possession, sin inclined nature, and the backsliding of his set apart nation. Healing by loosening is the process of breaking strongholds and bonds that cause backsliding. One of the most well-known processes for breaking strongholds is fasting.

> *Is not this the fast that I have chosen? to loose the bands of wickedness, to undo the heavy burdens, and to let the oppressed go free, and that ye break every yoke?*
>
> **Isaiah 58:6**

In the cycle of Yahuah's Feast days there is a specific feast set aside to afflict the soul. In this feast there is fasting and loosening of the sin into the desert on the scape goat. The process of loosening represents freedom from bondage. We see a perfect example of this loosening in the healing of one of the daughters of Abraham by Yahoshua in Luke 13:10-17.

> *And he was teaching in one of the synagogues on the sabbath. And, behold, there was a woman which had a spirit of infirmity eighteen years, and was bowed together, and could in no wise lift up herself. And when Jesus saw her, he called her to him, and said unto her, Woman, thou art loosed from thine infirmity. And he laid his hands on her: and immediately she was made straight, and glorified God. And the ruler of the synagogue answered with indignation, because that Jesus had healed on the sabbath day, and said unto the people, There are six days in which men ought to work: in them therefore come and be*

healed, and not on the sabbath day. The Lord then answered him, and said, Thou hypocrite, doth not each one of you on the sabbath loose his ox or his ass from the stall, and lead him away to watering? And ought not this woman, being a daughter of Abraham, whom Satan hath bound, lo, these eighteen years, be loosed from this bond on the sabbath day? And when he had said these things, all his adversaries were ashamed: and all the people rejoiced for all the glorious things that were done by him.

Healing by Words

Just as the tapestry is repaired with new fabric, Israel is repaired with new flesh. This new flesh is the new heart (of flesh) where Yahuah will write his words which are healing.

And I will give them one heart, and I will put a new spirit within you; and I will take the stony heart out of their flesh, and will give them an heart of flesh:

Ezekiel 11:19

Circumcise therefore the foreskin of your heart, and be no more stiffnecked.

Deuteronomy 10:16

"In that day I will restore the fallen tent of David. I will repair its gaps, restore its ruins, and rebuild it as in the days of old"

Amos 9:11

Another word which pertains to the healing of the Nation of Israel is *malah* (מלה). *Malah* means, "to fill," "speak a word," or a "statement through careful consideration in order to bind up an ailment or affliction." Another cognate of the word *malah*

(מלה) is מול which means, "to circumcise" or "to cause something to cease by making an oath." Just a word from Yahuah is enough to bind up the enemies of Israel as well as heal the nation. We see this exact same function in the Messiah. When the Messiah came, he spoke to demons and they were cast out, he cured illness, prophesied, and raised the dead by his Word. Proverbs 18:21 tells us:

> *Death and life are in the power of the tongue: and they that love it shall eat the fruit thereof.*

The words that we utter can bring life which is necessary in the restoration of the unified Israelite Nation. As a people we have endured a plethora of discrimination both within and without. The House of Judah in particular has been stigmatized and rejected on the sheer basis of skin and the curse of slavery which *she* still bears the mark of to this day. As a people there is a war from within and an enemy without. In the restoration and the joining together it is prophesied that we will no longer be at odds with one another. There will be no more vexation but unity (Isaiah 11:13, Ezekiel 37:16-17, Jeremiah 50:4).

> *The envy also of Ephraim shall depart, and the adversaries of Judah shall be cut off: Ephraim shall not envy Judah, and Judah shall not vex Ephraim.*
> **Isaiah 11:13**

Now more than ever, it is crucial that we wash one another in the Word of Truth and that we speak LIFE to one another. One of the issues of a disenfranchised nation is the downcast mind, lack of love, and endless arguments trying to prove who is right instead of doing what is right. Ezekiel was told to prophesy to the wind so that they Ruach could enter the dry bones so that they could live. That utterance was life-giving and showed the restoration of the Nation through the Ruach. To bring healing which is by definition, to restore a person in good health and relationship with the Creator, a person has to proclaim the Truth of Yah's Word over His people.

> To the law and to the testimony: if they speak not according to this word, it is because there is no light in them.
>
> **Isaiah 18:20**

When we restore one another then Yah will restore us. This restoration comes when we *fill* each other with careful speech, when our words to one another are not words of vexation, and words of healing act as evidence of transformation because of the Covenant. Our words as a nation are no longer our own words but are the proclamation of truth and love from Yahuah over his people.

> Let the word of Messiah dwell in you richly in all wisdom; teaching and admonishing one another in psalms and hymns and spiritual songs, singing with grace in your hearts to the Lord.
>
> **Colossians 3:16**

> "Thy words have upholden him that was falling, and thou hast strengthened the feeble knees."
>
> **Job 4:4**

> The words of Yah have upheld the one who was fallen and strengthened him.
>
> **Psalm 145:14**

The circumcision of our hearts should also lead to the circumcision of our lips. Our speech should be transformed as we heal. We should no longer speak words of low degree but should be uplifting with words of exaltation. Each person seeking wholeness must understand that restoration is in the Covenant and in the Words which Yahuah has given. No man does anything by his own power, but everything is done by the power and will of Elohim to His Glory.

In Jeremiah 30, Yah says he will heal the land of Israel and restore them. We must align. As stated before, the earth awaits the revelation of the sons and daughters of Israel. Our healing comes in the light of Yah's covenant.

> *"For the earnest expectation of the creature waiteth for the manifestation of the* **Sons of Elohim**. *For the creature was made subject to vanity, not willingly, but by reason of him who hath subjected the same in hope, Because the creature itself also shall be delivered from the bondage of corruption into the glorious liberty of the children of Elohim. For we know that the whole creation groaneth and travaileth in pain together until now. And not only they, but ourselves also, which have the firstfruits of the Spirit, even we ourselves groan within ourselves, waiting for the adoption, to wit, the redemption of our body."*
>
> **Romans 8:19-23**

Healing is one of the means by which faith is strengthened. Healing is meant to take the attention away from the individual and bring glory to Yah. It will be in the healing and restoration that Israel will be known. When we are made whole the final fulfillment of Yahuah's Prophecy concerning the disenfranchised state of Israel will be brought to light.

> *The sons of your oppressors will come and bow down to you; all who reviled you will fall facedown at your feet and call you the City of Yahuah, Zion of the Holy One of Israel.*
>
> **Isaiah 60:14**

Behold, I will make them of the synagogue of Satan, which say they are Jews, and are not, but do lie; behold, I will make them to come and worship before thy feet, and to know that I have loved thee.

Revelation 3:9

But I will restore your health and heal your wounds, declares Yahuah, because they call you an outcast, Zion, for whom no one cares."

Jeremiah 30:17

Praise ye Yahuah. Praise Yahuah, O my soul. While I live will I praise Yahuah: I will sing praises unto my Elohim while I have any being. Put not your trust in princes, nor in the son of man, in whom there is no help. His breath goeth forth, he returneth to his earth; in that very day his thoughts perish. Happy is he that hath the Elohim of Jacob for his help, whose hope is in Yahuah his Elohim: Which made heaven, and earth, the sea, and all that therein is: which keepeth truth for ever: Which executeth judgment for the oppressed: which giveth food to the hungry. Yahuah looseth the prisoners: Yahuah openeth the eyes of the blind: Yahuah raiseth them that are bowed down: Yahuah loveth   the righteous: Yahuah preserveth the strangers; he relieveth the fatherless and widow: but the way of the wicked he turneth upside down. Yahuah shall reign for ever, even thy Elohim, O Zion, unto all generations. Praise ye Yahuah.

Psalm 146

But ye are a chosen generation, a royal priesthood, an holy nation, a peculiar people; that ye should shew forth the praises of him who hath called you out of darkness into his marvellous light:

1 Peter 2:19

Epilogue: Israel's Brilliance

You are the light of the world because Yah is the light of the world. Yah's word is light so if His word is in us then the world shall be illuminated by us. We are Light Bearers.

> *For ye were sometimes darkness, but now are ye light in the Lord: walk as children of light: (For the fruit of the Spirit is in all goodness and righteousness and truth;) Proving what is acceptable unto the Lord. And have no fellowship with the unfruitful works of darkness, but rather reprove them. For it is a shame even to speak of those things which are done of them in secret. But all things that are reproved are made manifest by the light: for whatsoever doth make manifest is light. Wherefore he saith, awake thou that sleepest, and arise from the dead, and Christ shall give thee light. See then that ye walk circumspectly, not as fools, but as wise, Redeeming the time, because the days are evil.*

Ephesians 5:8-16

No man, when he hath lighted a candle, putteth it in a secret place, neither under a bushel, but on a candlestick, that they which come in may see the light. The light of the body is the eye: therefore when thine eye is single, thy whole body also is full of light; but when thine eye is evil, thy body also is full of darkness. Take heed therefore that the light which is in thee be not darkness. If thy whole body therefore be full of light, having no part dark, the whole shall be full of light, as when the bright shining of a candle doth give thee light.

Luke 11:33-36

While ye have light, believe in the light, that ye may be the children of light. These things spake Yahoshua, and departed, and did hide himself from them.

John 12:36

Again, a new commandment I write unto you, which thing is true in him and in you: because the darkness is past, and the true light now shineth.

1 John 2:8

The last days will be as the days of Noah (Matthew 24:37-39). One family with one focus, operating amongst the darkness of the world. Normally when we focus on this story, we look at the condition of the world and abandon the acts of the righteous. The beauty of the story was a unified group willing to do the will of Yahuah in order to provide a place of safety and sanctuary for the whole world. As the *Children of Light*, our light, was intended to penetrate through the darkness of the world and to be a beacon to those lost and wandering. Many of us have reclaimed our *stolen* identity. This prophesied reclamation requires us to also walk in our role as an ensign to the nations. The Nation of Israel has become an ARK. The Ark built by Noah was a place of refuge from judgment and the ARK of the Nation of Israel represents invitation into a place of protection before the destruction of the world. Time is winding up and there is still work to be done (John 9:4), messages to be preached (2 Timothy 2:4-2), and a nation to be gathered (Isaiah 11:12). Now is not the time to hide our light rather it is time to fully illuminate and walk in the wholeness that is provided through the gift from the Bridegroom our Savior.

For this work to take place we must be ONE and the only way to be ONE is in the example of the Word made flesh. We have to walk out the ways of Messiah. We must follow after him to know what unity looks like, even in the face of adversity. Our kinsman redeemer prayed that we would be ONE as he is ONE with Abba Yah. This unity is rooted in the will of Yah.

> *"Now I beseech you, brethren, by the name of our Master Yahoshua Messiah, that ye all speak the same thing, and that there be no divisions among you; but that ye be perfectly joined together in the same mind and in the same judgment."*
> **1 Corinthians 1:10**

> *"That they all may be ONE; as thou, Father, art in me, and I in thee, that they also may be ONE in us: that the world may believe that thou hast sent me."*
> **John 17:21**

It is time that we consider one another, put away foolish and selfish motivation and unify. Our gifts are evident, our talents are present, but our oneness is lacking. Our western mind has caused us to seek knowledge and neglect service. Everyone is teaching and gaining knowledge but very few are serving. We are the bride, and we have to focus and prepare. We have to allow the Ruach to help us manifest the gifts and lead us into all truth.

"But the Comforter, which is the Ruach HaKodesh, whom the Father will send in my name, he shall teach you all things, and bring all things to your remembrance, whatsoever I have said unto you."

John 14:26

Israel's Gifts Matter

We live in a time when people are struggling to believe in Yah because of the conditions of the world. Because of death, destruction, and natural disaster, people have come to deny and even loathe the idea of a Creator. What if the issue with the world was not Yah but creation? What if we were supposed to be the Elohim of the earth, healing and being the visible image of Yah, and we have dropped the ball. Our current world condition is evidence of the dysfunction and disenfranchisement of the *Elect*. You see, people always think they know better than Yah. All creation is in a chaotic spiral because of the removal, hiding, and denying of Yah's people through replacement theology and crafty counsel (Psalm 83).

I once watched a children's movie called "Home." In the Movie, an alien nation was on the path to destroy the world. Everyone thought the destroyers were "evil." In the end, it was revealed that the world set for destruction had stolen a relic and was using it for their own selfish gain. Inside the relic were all of the babies (seed) of the *alien* nation, and they were going to die if they didn't recover them! Sound familiar? Nations around the world are holding Elohim's Seed. They are being oppressed and used to advance their cults, entertainment industry, sick, and selfish desires. All the while, the world is falling apart because the people that that Yah designated to be the light of the world are being used for everything *except* Yah's Glory. If someone doesn't come and save us, we will eventually flicker out and be no more.

> And except those days should be shortened, there should no flesh be saved: but for the elect's sake those days shall be shortened.
>
> **Matthew 24:22**

> And shall not Yahuah avenge His *own elect*, which cry day and night unto Him, though He bear long with them? I tell you that He will avenge them speedily. Nevertheless, when the Son of Man cometh, shall he find faith on the earth?
>
> **Luke 18:7-8**

In order to be redeemed we have to focus on the present. So many of us are caught up in figuring out the past and unraveling the prophecy of the future that we are mismanaging the present. It is our present responsibility to be restored to the Father in love.

> *"By this shall all men know that ye are my disciples, if ye have love one to another."*
>
> **John 15:35**

If we want to see change in the world then the Light Bearers must *illuminate*. We must unify in Messiah, understand our function, put aside all fruitlessness and stand on the Truth of Torah. It is time for the Brilliance of Yah in Israel to come forth. May the words of Messiah and those of the apostle Paul to the assembly at Thessalonica comfort you and give you shalom (peace, wholeness, wellness) in your endeavor to walk in the fullness of your calling.

But the Comforter, which is the Ruach HaKodesh, whom the Father will send in my name, he shall teach you all things, and bring all things to your remembrance, whatsoever I have said unto you. Peace I leave with you, my peace I give unto you: not as the world giveth, give I unto you. Let not your heart be troubled, neither let it be afraid.

John 14:26-27

---

*Ye are all the children of **light**, and the children of the **day**: we are not of the night, nor of darkness. Therefore, let us not sleep, as do others; but let us watch and be sober. For they that sleep sleep in the night; and they that be drunken are drunken in the night. But let us, who are of the **day**, be sober, putting on the breastplate of faith and love; and for an helmet, the hope of salvation. For Elohim hath not appointed us to wrath, but to obtain salvation by our Master Yahoshua Messiah, who died for us, that, whether we wake or sleep, we should live together with him. Wherefore comfort yourselves together, and edify one another, even as also ye do. And we beseech you, brethren, to know them which labour among you, and are over you in Yahuah, and admonish you; And to esteem them very highly in love for their work's sake. And be at peace among yourselves. Now we exhort you, brethren, warn them that are unruly, comfort the feebleminded, support the weak, be patient toward all men. See that none render evil for evil unto any man; but ever follow that which is good, both among yourselves, and to all men.*

Rejoice evermore.

Pray without ceasing.

In everything give thanks: for this is the will of Elohim in Messiah Yahoshua concerning you.

Quench not the Spirit.

Despise not prophesyings.

Prove all things; hold fast that which is good.

Abstain from all appearance of evil.

And the very Elohim of peace sanctify you wholly; and I pray Elohim your whole spirit and soul and body be preserved blameless unto the coming of our Master Yahoshua Messiah.

Faithful is he that calleth you, who also will do it.

Brethren, pray for us.

1 Thessalonians 5:5-25

DICTIONARY OF SPIRITUAL GIFTS

This Dictionary is a non-exhaustive list of the Gifts of the Spirit found in the Bible. The majority of words were obtained from the New testament texts pertaining to Gifts of the Spirit and traced back to their Hebrew origin using the Septuagint text (LXX).

How to use this Dictionary:

The words in this dictionary are defined in English, Greek, and Hebrew. All of the explanations of the gifts are done using the Hebrew language as the guide for function. We chose this method because it is the authors belief that the Hebrew language is the foundation for all languages and gives the most concrete understanding of Biblical words. The reader will be able to view the most frequent translations and a brief definition in the chart. The Strong's # and Ancient Hebrew Lexicon numbers are provided to facilitate a more in-depth personal study.

Hebrew Equivalents:

Each Greek word has one or more Hebrew equivalent words. This provides cross-linguistic information concerning the LXX definitions used to translate from the Hebrew text into Greek. A single Greek word may be used to describe multiple Hebrew words. To keep this process consistent and to provide the reader with enough information there are several synonyms to help frame the understanding of each gift as intended by the Creator.

Linguistic Sources Used to Obtain Definitions:

The Lexham Analytical Lexicon to The Greek New Testament by Rick Brannan

The Greek-Hebrew Reverse Interlinear Septuagint: H.B. Swete Edition (GHRIS*)* by Chip McDaniel, Rick Brannan, Isaiah Hoogendyk

Dictionary of Biblical Languages with Semantic Domains (Greek, New Testament) by James A. Swanson

Theological Dictionary of The New Testament, Abridged in Volume 1 by Gerhard Kittel, Gerhard Friedrich, Geoffery William Bromiley

The Lexham Greek English Interlinear Septuagint by Randall Tan, David A deSilva

Etymological Dictionary of Biblical Hebrew by Matityahu Clark

Ancient Hebrew Lexicon of The Bible by Jeff Benner

Strong's Exhaustive Concordance by James Strong

106

ADMINISTRATION – κυβέρνησις[17] (kybernēsis)

Administrator is defined as one who keeps a system bound together and directs and rules. The Administrator "steers" and "governs" the people into the direction that Yahuah chooses. Individuals skilled in this area are gifted in implementation of plans concerning the kingdom as well as leading others in using their gifts to complete a task or meet a goal which has been set forth. The individual with this gift must also be able to give wise counsel and uses that wise counsel to bind the collective. Their compassion causes them to nurture and to guide as one who draws their beloved ones into their bosom to instruct them and guide them with love and care (Isaiah 40:11).

Pro 1:15, Ezekiel 27:29, Luke 14:28-30, Acts 6:1-7 I Corinthians 12:28

Hebrew Equivalent from LXX: תַּחְבֻּלוֹת (immediately derived from the nouns חֶבֶל a rope, חֹבֵל)

	Root word	Strong's/AHLB	Definition
תַּחְבֻּלוֹת	חֶבֶל	Strong's #8458 AHLB #2141	To bind something by wrapping it around with ropes.

NOTES:

_____

_____

_____

[17] Cognate word: κυβερνήτης

<u>APOSTLESHIP</u> – ἀπόστολος (Apostolos)

An apostle is a messenger on who carries a message on the behalf of another. The function of an apostle is to make known, announce, and to inform the people of the word of Yahuah.

Genesis 32:6, Joshua 6:25, 1 Samuel 6:20, Obadiah 1:1, Acts 15:1-2 I Corinthians 12:28 II Corinthians 12:12 Galatians 2:7-10 Ephesians 3:1-9 Ephesians 4:11-14

Hebrew Equivalent from LXX: מלאך, נגד, בשר, ציר

	Root word	Strong's/AHLB	Definition
ציר	ציר	Strong's#1913, 1914 AHLB #1411	The produce of a hunter.
בשר	בשר	Strong's#1319 AHLB #2025	When meat is prepared to celebrate good news at a feast.
נגד	נגד	Strong's#5046 AHLB #2372	One who tells orders or gives an account to another.
מלאך	מלך	Strong's#4397 AHLB #2340	To reign over a kingdom or walk amongst the people.

NOTES:

_____

_____

_____

_____

CRAFTSMANSHIP – מְלָאכָה

A craftsman is one who is diligent in his business. An individual who labors and works with their hands or is occupied to do work or labor. Yahuah in Genesis 2:2 wrought creation into existence with his wisdom. A workman is one who creates and brings to fruition the desires of Yahuah through the interpretation and wisdom of the Ruach HaKodesh. This can be in building or designing a designated space. This can also be an individual who creates beaten works of precious metals or art for the kingdom. This particular gift requires careful consideration of the will of Yah and how that is to be expressed in all the work that the workman creates.

1 Timothy 5:18, Exodus 30:22-25 Exodus 31:3-11, Exodus 35:31, II Chronicles 34:9-13 Acts 18:2-3, Matthew 16:21-23

NOTES:

_____

_____

_____

_____

_____

_____

_____

_____

DISCERNMENT – διάκρισις

The cognitive process of knowing the difference between two or more stimuli or objects. To judge or pass judgment through careful consideration of individual actions or circumstances. The gift of discernment allows an individual to judge the contents or appraise the worth of the inward parts of a person to determine if their ways are of Yahuah or not. To look at the word of Yah and discern and look at the proper outcome or judgment of a situation.

Genesis 18:19, Ezekiel 44:24, Deuteronomy 1:17, proverbs 29:26, Acts 5:1-11, Acts 16:16-18, I Corinthians 12:10, I John 4:1-6

Hebrew Equivalent from LXX: דעת, סכל, בין, מִשְׁפָּט

	Root word	Strong's/AHLB	Definition
מִשְׁפָּט	שָׁפַט	Strong's #4941, 4942, 8239, 8240 AHLB #2870	To judge, create order, or harmony. To set in place.
בין	בין	Strong's #995 AHLB #1037	One who has insight or understands reason through knowledge.
סכל	סכל	Strong's #5528, 7919, 7922, 7924 AHLB #2477	One who can consider and comprehend a situation to make a prosperous decision
דעת	דעת	Strong's #1847 AHLB #1085A	A knowledge focused on moral qualities.

NOTES:

_____

_____

EVANGELISM - εὐαγγελίζω (euangelizō)

An evangelist is responsible for proclaiming the covenant. A covenant is established over the death of an animal. This covenant symbolized what would happen to either party at the breaking of the covenant. The evangelist is one who tells of the covenant agreement between Israel and their creator and the good news that he has provided a lamb for their breaking of the covenant which ratified and renewed the previously rent relationship between them and their creator.

Genesis 17:10, Isaiah 40:9, Isaiah 41:27, Psalm 68:12, Nahum 2:1, Acts 8:5-6 Acts 8:26-40 Acts 14:21 Acts 21:8 Ephesians 4:11-14 II Timothy 4:5

Hebrew Equivalent from LXX: בשׂר

	Root word	Strong's/AHLB	Definition
בשׂר	בשׂר	Strong's # 1319 AHLB # 2025	Heralding; bringing a message.

NOTES:

_____

_____

_____

_____

_____

_____

EXHORTATION/HELPS – ἀντίλημψις (*antilēmpsis*)

One of the characteristics of Yahuah is a helper or one who helps and assists (Genesis. 49:25). Exhortation means to help, assist, or to act. Exhortation means to keep one to their task through the process of support. This is more than a help of mental agreement; it is a help of rescue and to run away enemies who are pursuing the one who has been placed into the care of the guardian. Just as Yahuah fights off the enemies of his people, it is necessary for the elect to uphold and rescue those of the body who fall into physical and spiritual distress thus putting them back into their place of service and worship.

Taking up or grasping. To enter into alliance with. For one to take up the cause of. One whom helps to keep one to the call (Isaiah 26:3) Helping in a reciprocal way. To cause one to bear fruit. Help those of the community to achieve what Yah has done in you. To be a strong and fortified place of defense. To be a fortress. To stand as a place of protection, refuge, and safety. To be a place of restoration and peace for those who become weary. To help someone become strengthened and bring them into safety. This is also a boldness and a sureness.

Genesis 49:2, Genesis 49:24, Exodus 6:6, Exodus 15:2, Deuteronomy 33:27, Proverbs 31:17, Proverbs 5:19 (Referring to a Wife as a place of fortress) Song of Sol. 2:7 (for women to guard herself from a man until he is ready for her) Proverbs 22:20, Isaiah 40:11, Luke 1:54, Acts 20:35, Ephesians 4:11-14, Isaiah 26:3, Isaiah 40:10-11, Isaiah 63:5, Psalm 37:17, 2 Samuel 22:31, Psalm 18:34

Hebrew Equivalent from LXX: (אול), אֱיָלוּת (איל), אַיָּלָה (עזז) מָעוֹז, מָגֵן, זְרוֹעַ

116

	Root word	Strong's/AHLB	Definition
אֱיָלוּת אַיָּלָה	אֱיָל	Strong's #360 AHLB #1012	One who strengthens. Seen as the older ox or a pillar that supports a building
זְרוֹעַ	זְרַע	Strong's #2220 AHLB#1158	To conceive. To spread or throw seed as the heads of grain are thrown into the wind and the seed falls to the ground where it can be scattered.
מָגֵן	מָגֵן	Strong's #4043 AHLB#1279, 2331	To guard or shield (a message).
עָזַז	עָזַז	Strong's #5810 AHLB #1352	To strengthen/ to be powerful. To be made hard or firm.

NOTES:

_____

_____

_____

_____

_____

_____

_____

_____

FAITH - πίστις (pistis)

The ability for one to be steadfast and chaste in the call and service to the Creator. One who is dependable and trustworthy (a pillar). One who knows truth and upholds the truth of the word. (See page 45 for further information).

Genesis 15:6, Exodus 4:31, Num 12:7, Acts 11:22-24 Romans 4:18-21 I Corinthians 12:9 Hebrews 11

Hebrew Equivalent from LXX: אֲמָנָה, אמן, אֱמֶת, אֱמוּנָה

	Root word	Strong's/AHLB	Definition
אֱמוּנָה	אֱמן	Strong's #530 AHLB #1290	To be a firm pillar. Something that grabs hold or supports something else.
אֱמֶת	אֱמֶת	Strong's #571 AHLB #1290-C	One who's arms hold the family together.

NOTES:

_____

_____

_____

_____

_____

_____

_____

GIVING – μεταδίδωμι (metadidōmi)

To give means to break or to shatter the outer of grain in order to surrender the tender, usable, edible portion on the inside. Giving is the breaking or distributing of gifts, talents, and resources in order to further the work wellness of the community. Giving can also be defined as exchanging currency or bartering with someone for resources, goods, or services. In community it is normal to communicate to one another through the exchange of monetary gifts and goods which one perceives is needed by the other. When something is broken up it is often to share or to distribute to those in need. Likewise, when community members give there is a dividing of resources for the benefit of the collective. Another definition of giving is the giving of one's worship and praise to another. The gifts and abilities of an individual should be dedicated, through worship and proper use, to the one who gave the gifts. It is imperative to be led by Yahuah in how we give our gifts and to whom we give our worship.

Exodus 23:24, Genesis 41:56, Mark 12:41-44 Romans 12:8 II Corinthians 8:1-7 II Corinthians 9:2-8

Hebrew Equivalent from LXX: שׁבר

	Root word	Strong's/AHLB	Definition
שׁבר	שׁבר	Strong's#7665 AHLB # 2811	The bursting out of crushed grain on the threshing floor.

NOTES:

_____

_____

120

HEALING – ἴαμα

The literal definition of healing means to shine light into dark places with words, confession, holistic health, and repairing the body, mind, and soul. An herbalist uses the Ruach and the understanding of herbs and the function of the body as revealed in Torah to bring the body back into alignment. This alignment is not just the ridding of disease but the cultivating of a repentant mind in order to help the individual cease from the behavior which led to the initial imbalance. True healing is holistic and places the individual back into the position of being a light bearer for Yahuah.

Genesis 1:11, Esther 8:16, Isaiah 26:19, Acts 3:1-10 Acts 5:12-16 Acts 9:32-35 Acts 28:7-10, I Corinthians 12:9,28

Hebrew Equivalent from LXX: מְלָה, אֲרוּכָה, אוֹרָה

	Root word	Strong's/AHLB	Definition
אוֹרָה	אוֹר	Strong's#219 AHLB #1020	To be light or to bring light.
מְלָה	מְלָה	Strong's#4405 AHLB #1288	To fill or permeate. To speak a word.
עֹז	עֹז	Strong's#5797 AHLB #1363	The uprightness or firmness of a tree.

NOTES:

_____

_____

_____

HOSPITALITY – φιλόξενος[18]

Hebrew hospitality extends beyond opening one's door and providing food although these are imperative to proper hospitality. True Hebraic hospitality is to call out and offer refuge and protection from the world without. This gift is both physical (to be carried out in our homes for those Yah chooses) and spiritual because Israel is a nation is established to show forth the glory of Yahuah to the nations. Hospitality is not one sided. Hospitality requires the individual who extending hospitality to prepare their home and family for the service of hospitality. Likewise, the one who is invited in must abide by the rules of the house which they enter and prepare themselves for the kindness which they will receive.

Genesis 18, Acts 16:14-15, Romans 12:9-13, Romans 16:23, Hebrews 13:1-2, I Peter 4:9

Hebrew Equivalent from LXX: for ξένος: מרט, גֵּר, נָכְרִי, קרא

Hebrew Equivalent from LXX: for φίλος: שַׂר, אהב, רֵעַ, שָׁלוֹם, שָׁכֵן, רֵעֶה, רֵעַ, ידע, חָכָם, מֵרֵעַ, אַלּוּף

	Root word	Strong's/AHLB	Definition
רֵעַ	רֵעַ	Strong's #7452 AHLB #1453	One who watches as a shepherd watched his sheep.
אהב	אהב	Strong's #157 AHLB #	To offer or bring forth. To express devotion to another.

---

[18] A compound of ξένος and φίλος

שֹׁר	שֹׁר	Strong's #8269 AHLB #1480	Fibers twisted together to create a rope that is used to tightly secure or support something.
אַלוּף	אלף	Strong's #502 AHLB #	To guide, yoke, or learn. As an older ox is yoked to a younger ox to teach it how to pull the load. To receive from others.
מֵרֵעַ	מֵרֵעַ	Strong's #4828 AHLB #	A friend or an advisor with a close association or who one has regard for.

NOTES:

_____

_____

_____

_____

_____

_____

_____

_____

_____

KNOWLEDGE - γνῶσις (gnōsis)

Knowledge is obtained through an intimate knowing of the Creator and his word. This requires experiencing and walking with Elohim. It is through this intimate knowledge that the believer is able to seek out the heart of Yahuah for their life. Without knowing Yahuah one is unable to know themselves. The knowledge of Creation is tied to an imitate relationship with its Creator. The knowledge gathered is then put into action and carried out in a way that glorifies Yahuah.

Genesis 3:5, Genesis 18:19, Proverbs 3:6, Psalm 19:1-2, Lev 5:4, Acts 5:1-11 I Corinthians 12:8 II Corinthians 11:6, Colossians 2:2-3

Hebrew Equivalent from LXX: רָעָה, רַע, יֹדע, דֵּעָה, דַּעַת, דֶּרֶךְ, דַּעַת

	Root word	Strong's/AHLB	Definition
דַּעַת	דַּעַת	Strong's#1847 AHLB #1085	To have an intimate relationship with another person, idea, or an experience.
יֹדע	יֹדע	Strong's#3045 AHLB #1085	To have an intimate relationship with another person, idea, or an experience.
רָעָה	רָעָה	Strong's#7451, 7462, 7465, 7473 AHLB #1453	A close companion who watches.
דֶּרֶךְ	דֶּרֶךְ	Strong's#1870 AHLB #2112	The path of life.

NOTES:

LANGUAGES/TONGUES - γλῶσσα (*glōssa*)

Kinds of tongues in (1 Corinthians 12:10) literally translate as *Geno-* "nation or people" *Glossa-* "tongue". This is a tongue which is spoken by a particular nation or people. The purpose of language is to communicate using a verbal code understood as speech. The speaking of tongues in the biblical sense can be understood in a few ways; as a language spoken by nations of the earth, as an angelic or divine tongue spoken by the messengers or angels of Elohim (Hebrew), also, similar to the first, an understood language, spoken by an individual with no previous knowledge of the language before they were divinely inspired to speak it. Language or tongues can also be a wordless melody either played on an instrument or hummed by divine inspiration.

- This gift is not required as proof of having the Ruach.
- This is not a gift given to everyone (1 Corinthians 12:30)
- Tongues can be languages found in the earth but can also be wordless utterances such as a niggun or sorrowful expression or deep prayer (1 Samuel 1:13-16, 1 Corinthians 14:2)
- Tongues are not the repetition of syllables and sounds evoked by religious ecstasy. Tongues are orderly (1 Corinthians 14:27-28, 33, 39-40).
- Tongues should not be spoken without an interpreter or an interpretation given (1 Corinthians 14:27-28)

Human misunderstanding of tongues and misuse of tongues in religious ceremony does not negate the gift of the Ruach used to speak to all peoples and the divine inspiration to speak the words of scripture (1 Corinthians 14:39). It should also be noted that Yahuah and the Ruach are the same, which means that the words spoken through the Ruach should align with the written word of scripture. This is how all gifts are tested. (1 Peter 4:11, Matthew 10:20)

Genesis 10:5, Exodus 4:10, Mark 16:17 Acts 2:1-13 Acts 10:44-46 Acts 19:1-7

Hebrew Equivalent from LXX: לָשׁוֹן, נָגַן, שָׁפַט, כָּבוֹד

	Root word	Strong's/AHLB	Definition
לָשׁוֹן	לֹשֶׁן	Strong's #3956 AHLB #2325	As coming from the movement of the tongue.
נָגַן	נָגַן	Strong's #5059 AHLB #2374	The bright sound of music/ to play a musical instrument.
שָׁפַט	שָׁפַט	Strong's #8202 AHLB #2864	To judge, create order, or harmony. To set in place.

NOTES:

_____

_____

_____

_____

_____

_____

_____

_____

LEADERSHIP – προΐστημι

There are various rulers in the scripture. Each position has a function. Some of the roles will overlap but each of them is imperative to the community. Leaders of households, community, fellowship, all require a heart of seeing, being an example, living out the word and following the laws statues and commandments of Abba Yah to the edification of the Body of the Messiah.

A leader sets goals in accordance with Yah's purpose for the future and communicates those goals to others in such a way that they voluntarily and harmoniously work together to accomplish those goals for the glory of Yah. Below is a list of each form of leadership. Please take some time to look at the roles that pertain to you, your home, and your call.

Genesis 42:6, Genesis 37:19, Genesis 49:26, Ex 16:22, Pro 6:7

Hebrew Equivalent from LXX: נגיד, שֹׂר, קָצִין, נשׂיא, סגן, רזן, נדיב, שלׂיט, בעל, נזיר, משל

	Root word	Strong's/AHLB	Definition
נשׂיא* *This word is also spelled with a samech	נשׂא	Strong's #4984, 5375, 5379, 7721 AHLB # 1314	One who lifts up the standard. A person who carries the load and is an example. One who is appointed to compel others to perform.
קָצִין	קצה	Strong's #7096, 7098 AHLB #1432	One who rules within a boarder. Head of society or a community.

שֹׂר	שֹׂר	Strong's #8269 AHLB #1342	A cord that binds the community. When the shin is changed to the samech it means one who turns the heads of the people in his direction. Chieftain, prince, commander.
נגיד	נגד	Strong's #5057 AHLB #2372	to give orders, inform, or provide an explanation. One who is the head of the family or a leader.
משל	משל	Strong's #4910 4911 AHLB #2359	To rule or have dominion and to judge or measure an issue.
נזיר	נזר	Strong's #5139 AHLB #2390	To be consecrated and devoted. A person who warns others to separate. A person set apart for a certain purpose.
בעל	בעל	Strong's #1169 AHLB #2027	One who is bound to a servant or to a particular job or task by a yoke. This word can also mean husband or master.
שליט	שלט	Strong's #7989,7990 AHLB #2843	One who is a master and has rule or dominion over someone.
נדיב	נדב	Strong's #5801 AHLB #2380	An individual who is willing, generous, and has a heart inclined toward the people. Volunteering help.
רזן	רזן	Strong's #7336	To be honorable and to rule.

		AHLB #2758	
סגן	סגן	Strong's #5461	One who is perfect.
		AHLB #2466	

NOTES:

_____

_____

_____

_____

_____

_____

_____

_____

MERCY - ἐλεέω

Mercy is the ability to feel compassion and to comfort those in need. One who expresses the beauty of Yahuah in their service and treatment of others. One who sees the soul of mankind and pities those who are in danger and acts in accordance with the word of Yahuah to admonish and aid them in their redemptive process. Showing mercy to a person has the ability to change their attitude and draw them into repentance. When the mercy of Yahuah is shown it is like taking a person into the womb of healing and guarding them as they go through their process of rebirth and renewal.

Genesis 19:16, Genesis 12:16, Genesis 49:2, Genesis 33:11;19, 2 kings 13:23, Matthew 9:35,36 Mark 9:41, I Thes. 5:14

Hebrew Equivalent from LXX: לֹא ,חמל ,רחם ,חנן קבץ ,עַיִן ,יטב ,הדר ,נחם ,רֶחָמָה

	Root word	Strong's/AHLB	Definition
חנן	חנן	Strong's#2603 AHLB # 1175	To give or show beauty, mercy, or grace to another.
רחם	רחם	Strong's#7355 AHLB #2762	The bowels are the seat of compassion.
חמל	חמל	Strong's#2550, 2565 AHLB #2171	To have compassion on someone or something.

NOTES:

_____

_____

MIRACLES - δύναμις (dynamis)

The purpose of miracles is to gather the Multitude (Nation) under its Leader (Yahuah). Just as the heavenly hosts serve as a sign of the Glory of Yahuah, so does the strong nation who is brought together in their wholeness (Genesis 2:1). Miracles are performed by the power of Yahuah to strengthen His people and must be done in accordance with His will. The gift of miracles was not a permanent gift that an individual had (except Messiah) unlimited access to, rather when the individual was strengthen the miracle was performed to the glory of Yahuah. The miracles are to confirm the presence of Yahuah *with* His set apart people. Those who have this gift have an added task of ensuring that people don't follow them but that they point them to Yahuah from which their power comes. This power is the might of Yahuah Tsavaot (of hosts) who is breaking down the defenses of the enemy through His elect.

Zechariah 9:8, Psalm 103:21, Psalm 148:2, Exodus 7:4, Exodus 12:41 Acts 9:36-42 Acts 19:11-20 Acts 20:7-12 Romans 15:18-19 I Corinthians 12:10,28

Hebrew Equivalent from LXX: כֹּחַ, גְּבוּרָה, עֹז, חַיִל; צָבָא, אָוֶן, תַּעֲלֻמָה, צְבִיָּה, מַחֲנֶה, חַיִל, הָמוֹן, הוֹן, גִּבּוֹר, גָּדוּד, מַתָּנָה, מִלְחָמָה, מְאֹד, יהוה, יָדַע, יָד, חָלַץ, חַיִלְךָ, גֹּבַהּ, אֵל, צוֹבָה, פֶּלֶא, עֱזוּז, עָבַד, סְלָלָה

	Root word	Strong's/AHLB	Definition
צָבָא	צָבָא	Strong's#6633, 6635, 6643 AHLB # 1393	To develop an army as a wall of defense.
חַיִל	חַיִל	Strong's#2428, 2429, 381	To enable/ develop abilities or power. To bore through

		AHLB #1173	the enemy by strongly pressing in.
עֹז	עֹז	Strong's#5797 AHLB #1363	The uprightness or firmness of a tree.
גְּבוּרָה	גְּבַר	Strong's#1369, 1370 AHLB #2052	One who is successful in strength and authority.
כֹּחַ	כֹּחַ	Strong's#3581 AHLB #1238	To correct or chastise with a firm hand.
גְּדוּד	גָּדַד	Strong's#1417 AHLB #1050	To band together as a group for attacking or raiding. To cut something by slicing it.

NOTES:

_____

_____

_____

_____

_____

_____

_____

_____

*MUSIC

The ability to make one noise and one sound in praise and thanksgiving to Yahuah. The ability to use one's voice, play a musical instrument, or write songs to praise Yahuah and aid others in worship.

Deuteronomy 31:22, I Samuel 16:16 I Chronicles 16:41-42, II Chronicles 5:12-13, II Chronicles 34:12, Psalm 150

Hebrew Equivalent: זְמַר, דָּוִד, שִׁיר, עוּגָב, זָמִיר, נְגִינָה, שִׁגָּיוֹן, נֶבֶל

	Root word	Strong's/AHLB	Definition
נָגַן	נָגַן	Strong's #5059 AHLB # 2374	One who plays instrumental music.
שִׁיר	שִׁיר	Strong's #7891 AHLB #1480	One who sings out or expresses thoughts in poetic form.
חצצר	חצר	Strong's #2690 AHLB #2197	To blow trumpets as a sound of an alarm to go to the protection of the walled city.
יָדָה	יָדָה	Strong's #3034 AHLB #1211	The throwing out of the for throwing, praising, or confessing.
מִזְמוֹר	זמר	Strong's #4210 AHLB #2124	A psalm, song, or a melody of words.

עָגָב	עָגָב	Strong's# 5689 AHLB #2523	To have sensual/sexual desire for another. Lust.
דָּוִד	דָּוִד	Strong's# 1732 AHLB #1073	The boiling of liquid in a pot or passion for another person.
זמר	זמר	Strong's# 2167 AHLB #2124	The sound of an instrument when strings are plucked. Th plucking of fruit from the vine.

*נֶבֶל- guitar or vessel that resonates sound

NOTES:

_____

_____

_____

_____

_____

_____

_____

_____

_____

_____

PASTOR/SHEPHERD – ποιμήν (*poimēn*)

A shepherd is one who commits to carrying for and meeting the needs of the flock whom Yah has gathered with his own blood. The responsibility of the pastor is to feed the sheep of Yahuah with his set apart diet, his word and to watches over them with a careful eye. The pastor is a watchman of the people and guides them with a heart and desire toward their safety and well-being. The shepherd is to lead the people to the pasture, which is the word of Elohim,

Genesis 4:2, Psalm 23, John 10:1-18 Ephesians 4:11-14 I Timothy 3:1-7 I Peter 5:1-3

Hebrew Equivalent from LXX: בֵּית, רֵעַ, עֵ֫דֶר, רעה מִצְרַ֫יִם

	Root word	Strong's/AHLB	Definition
עֵ֫דֶר	עֵ֫דֶר	Strong's#5739, 5740 AHLB # 2530	Moving what is unnecessary to create order.
רעה	רעה	Strong's #7462, 7463 AHLB # 1453-H	

NOTES:

_____

_____

_____

_____

_____

PRAYERS/INTERCESSION–προσεύχομαι (proseuchomai)

Prayer is the means by which humans are allowed to speak to authority. The job of the intercessor is to come before the one in authority on behalf of another or for self. Prayer is the means by which man can agree or plead for mercy concerning the judgment of the Creator. Prayer begins from a swelling desire that only Yahuah can fulfill.

Genesis 9:26, Genesis 20:7, Genesis 25:21, Exodus 8:30, Num 11:2, Job 22:27, Job 33:26, 1 Kings 8:28-30, Ezra 6:10, Daniel 6:10-11, Luke 22:41-44 Acts 12:12 Colossians 1:9-12 Colossians 4:12-13 I Timothy 2:1-2 Acts 4:32-37 Acts 14:22 Romans 12:8 I Timothy 4:13 Hebrews 10:24-25

Hebrew Equivalent from LXX: פלל, עתר, צלה, בעה

	Root word	Strong's/AHLB	Definition
בעה	בעה	Strong's#1158 AHLB # 1039	One who seeks, request, or inquires. To swell up or boil.
צלה	צלה	Strong's#6740 AHLB #1403	To darken. A place of shadows. To roast completely over with flames.
עתר	עתר	Strong's#6282 AHLB #2590	To multiply or press strongly toward a goal.
פלל	פלל	Strong's#6419 AHLB #1380	To plead in intercession by coming to one in authority to intercede on one's own behalf or for another.

NOTES:

_____

_____

PROPHECY – προφητεία (prophēteia)

A prophet is a hollowed-out vessel through which the spirit of Yahuah speaks. The genuine prophet acts with the hand of Yahuah. The prophet is one who brings forth the seed from the fruit covering. There are false and true prophets. The false prophet brings forth the seed and the will of Satan, while the true prophet brings forth the truth of Yahs word which calls his people into obedience and repentance.

Acts 2:37-40; Acts 7:54; Acts 26:24-29; I Corinthians 14:1,3; I Thessalonians 1:5

Hebrew Equivalent from LXX: חֲזוֹן, נְבוּאָה, חֹזֶה

	Root word	Strong's/AHLB	Definition
חָזוֹן	חָזֹן	Strong's#2377 AHLB #	One with vision, seeing beyond what is seen in the physical. A light piercing through the darkness.
נְבָא	נְבָא	Strong's#5012, 5012 AHLB #1301	To speak the word of Yah. To bring forth inner fruit/ knowledge of something that is not known by the five senses.

NOTES:

_____

_____

_____

_____

_____

SERVICE - διάκονος[19] (diakonos)

A high communal service. Service is the activities or work assigned to or required of, and freely given from one to another. A person in service divides or shares a part of the whole task. In the body of Messiah this individual operates according to their call and role. This could be temple ministry, one who serves another in leadership, or a young person who serves. This service also includes the service of the stranger in the rebuilding of the walls of Jerusalem.

Genesis 39:4, Exodus 24:13, Num 3:31, Num 8:26, Deuteronomy 18:7, Nehemiah 4:10, 1Ch 27:1; 28:1-2, Isaiah 60:10, Acts 6:1-7 Romans 12:7 Galatians 6:2 II Timothy 1:16-18 Titus 3:14

Hebrew Equivalent from LXX: נַעַר ,שרת

	Root word	Strong's/AHLB	Definition
נַעַר	נַעַר	Strong's #5288, 5289 AHLB #2418	To be youthful.
שרת	שרת	Strong's #8334 AHLB #2884	To be in service to another.

NOTES:

_____

_____

_____

[19] Cognate words: διακονέω, διακονία

TEACHING – διδάσκω (didaskō)

The Biblical instructor teaches the student how to properly use and apply the knowledge and wisdom of Torah. The teacher helps the student train to hit the target (Yah's righteousness as established in Torah). The teacher also is the one who points and instructs the student in the direction of the Creator. This allows the student to use the information in the Scripture for practical use and to produce moral and ethical behavior. A teacher of the Word of Elohim teaches the student to consistently hit the standard of the Word. The student is yoked to the instructor who is charged with walking with and teaching the student and goading them into the right direction. Most importantly the teacher has to be the greatest student. The most effective teacher of the word is one who is consistently at the feet of Yahuah learning of him and having a submitted disposition to instruction and discipline through Torah.

Deuteronomy 4:1, Deuteronomy 31:12, Psalm 25:4-5, Psalm 34:11, Acts 18:24-28, Acts 20:20-21 I Corinthians 12:28

Hebrew Equivalent from LXX: (ירה) מורה ידע, למד

	Root word	Strong's/AHLB	Definition
למד	למד	Strong's#3925 AHLB #2311	The directing the path of the ox by goading it. To learn from practical use or ethical behavior.
ידע	ידע	Strong's#3045 AHLB #1211	The hand that can throw away grab hold of, kill or heal, make or destroy.
מורה	ירה	Strong's#4172, 4175 AHLB #1227	To throw your finger to show direction to walk or live. To teach. Inform, or instruct.

NOTES:

<u>WISDOM</u> – σοφία (sophia)

Words of wisdom are from a trained pallet. A trained pallet has been instructed to tell the difference between good and bad, function and dysfunction, and the sweetness of the word as compared to the bitterness of deceit. It is through commandments of Yahuah and the walking therein that causes a person to speak and act under the influence of the Ruach. Wisdom is accumulated through experience and training in the word of Yahuah. Through this training a person is enlightened and able to discern and perform with skill and precision the will of Yah.

Deuteronomy 4:6, Psalm 119:98, Psalm 19:7, Proverbs 1:4, Proverbs 4:1, 2 Timothy 3:15, Acts 6:3,10 I Corinthians 2:1-13 I Corinthians 12:8 James 1:5 II Peter 3:15

Hebrew Equivalent from LXX: חָכְמָה

	Root word	Strong's/AHLB	Definition
חָכְמָה	חָכַם	Strong's#2451, 2452, 2454 AHLB #2159	To be wise.

NOTES:

_____

_____

_____

_____

_____

ABOUT THE AUTHOR

Huldah is a Malagasy Hebrew descendant. It is the oral tradition of her family that they were taken from Madagascar on a Dutch slave ship to Holland. It was from Holland that her family made it to North Carolina. Huldah has a master's degree in Education and is the founder of Her Royal Roots and Royal Roots Academy. She currently resides in California with her husband and two children. Her passion and focus are the liberation of women and children through truth of their rich cultural heritage.

Made in the USA
Middletown, DE
10 March 2021